100
CURIOSITIES
& INVENTIONS

From the Collections of the
National Trust

100 CURIOSITIES & INVENTIONS

From the Collections of the National Trust

KATIE KNOWLES

With entries by Helen Antrobus, Emma Campagnaro, Katherine Carter,
Hannah Mawdsley, Stephen Ponder, Alice Rylance-Watson and Harvey Wilkinson

 National Trust

Contents

Introduction

The National Trust cares for one of the most significant collections of fine-art and heritage objects in the world, but did you know this includes electric jewellery, Roman-era pawprints, a heliograph, boxing squirrels, hair earrings and even a Dalek? This book brings together a selection of little-known but remarkable objects in the collections that puzzle, intrigue and enchant 21st-century visitors, volunteers and staff. Together, these objects help us to understand the rich histories of the places in the Trust's care, and the lives and interests not just of those who owned them but of all those who lived and worked there.

From household gadgets and humorous gifts to personal treasures and ground-breaking technology, these curiosities and inventions were

Opposite · Sir Vauncey Harpur Crewe's bedroom at Calke Abbey, Derbyshire, with cabinets containing his extensive fossil and shell collections to the left.

Frontispiece · Detail of a *buccin à tête de dragon* (*c.*1800–30) from the collection of Charles Paget Wade at Snowshill, Gloucestershire (pages 98–9).

Pages 4–5 · Third of five cases showing pairs of stuffed red squirrels in boxing poses (*c.*1900) by Edward Hart at Castle Ward, County Down (pages 112–15).

prized for their ingenuity, distinctiveness and craftsmanship. Unlike most museum artefacts, the 100 objects featured in this book are often presented in their original contexts, in the places they were made, displayed, treasured and used. These places include grand country houses, such as Kedleston Hall and Kingston Lacy, but also gardens and landscapes, places of industry, such as Quarry Bank, and more modest homes, such as Townend and Sunnycroft. Other featured objects are associated with the homes of visionary thinkers or places where momentous discoveries were made that changed the way we live today, from Lacock Abbey to Woolsthorpe Manor. With such a broad historical and geo-graphical spread of properties and collections, the Trust is exceptionally well placed to consider the practical inventions and intriguing curiosities that have stemmed from centuries of innovation. Collectively, these objects can help to trace the history of social and technological changes that have affected us all.

Products of curiosity

For thousands of years humans have used their curiosity and creativity to shape the world around them and meet their changing needs. This desire for knowledge and eagerness to experiment has led to discoveries and inventions that transformed how people live, act and think. Some of these inventions met basic survival needs, while others helped humanity to make sense of an ever-changing world. As well as practical problem-solving, this inventiveness led to creative artistic experiments with unexpected materials and the emergence of new ideas.

As new technology developed, so did the ability to communicate ideas, knowledge and innovation through travel, printing and, later, through wireless and electronic communication. From the late 19th century, a great surge of scientific and technological development brought new discoveries and inventions, including synthetic materials (such as plastics), cars, radio, medicines and electric light, all of which are familiar features of our lives today. Many of the wealthy residents and owners of National Trust properties were early adopters of the latest technology, such as gadget-loving millionaire Julius Drewe (1856–1931) of Castle Drogo (pages 32–3), who proudly displayed his cutting-edge electrical devices to guests. The owner of Cragside, innovator William Armstrong (1810–1900), made his home into a showplace of technology, and it was the first private house in the world to be lit by hydroelectricity (page 22). Industrial entrepreneurs also made use of the latest technology, which paved the way for factories and mass production. For example,

soon after the patent on inventor Richard Arkwright's water-powered spinning machines lapsed in the 1780s, Samuel Greg (1758–1834) built Quarry Bank, using the technology to power his cotton factory and revolutionise his textile business (opposite and pages 156–9).

The National Trust also looks after a number of places where discoveries were made that helped to transform the modern world. It was at Woolsthorpe Manor that philosopher and mathematician Isaac Newton (1642–1727) made some of his most important discoveries, leaving traces of his genius on the walls (pages 188–9). Technology that paved the way for instant, world-wide communication was tested by Italian inventor Guglielmo Marconi (1874–1937) on The Lizard peninsula in Cornwall and St Catherine's Point on the Isle of Wight. At Lacock Abbey, William Fox Talbot (1800–77) invented the negative, a photographic process that fixed images on paper. Other places were home to creative thinkers who invented new worlds using their imagination. At Hill Top, the home of Beatrix Potter (1866–1943), visitors can still see some of the dolls' house toys that appear in her much-loved books and illustrations (pages 182–3), while at Bateman's a necklace created

Opposite · A creel or warping frame at Quarry Bank, Cheshire, which gathers up strands of yarn to be woven into cloth on a loom.

in the imagination of Rudyard Kipling (1865–1936) for one of his *Just So Stories* was brought to life by a talented craftsperson (pages 166–7).

Invention is not necessarily about coming up with a completely new idea. It can also be about improving or adapting an existing design. The following pages include a number of inventions that serve as a reminder of continual innovation and development in the 21st century. They include an early prosthetic limb at Cotehele (page 46) with adjustable fingers that gave the wearer modest use and movement. Thanks to continued improvement and research, modern prosthetics now exist that can be controlled by muscle movements. Some of the objects in this book are early examples of familiar items that we use every day and that have evolved for ease of use, such as the patent hairdryer at Wightwick Manor (page 53) and the portable shower at Erddig (pages 54–5). Sprinklers and fire extinguishers have replaced the Victorian glass grenade (page 27), but the modern perfume bottle can find its ancestor in the fragment of a Roman glass bottle at Chedworth (pages 104–5). Other objects, such as the glasses at Souter Lighthouse (pages 44–5), may have been adapted for a use beyond their original purpose.

Right · A selection of string, brass and wind instruments in the Music Room at Snowshill, Gloucestershire.

Collecting through time

Many of the world's oldest museums began as personal collections accumulated by wealthy families or individuals. In the 16th and 17th centuries, European collectors created cabinets of curiosities or *Wunderkammer* (wonder-rooms) to intrigue guests and demonstrate an understanding of the world around them. These could be cabinets, cupboards or entire rooms that brought together objects – both natural and manufactured – from around the world for study and display. Later generations created their own personal collections, from physical 'cabinets' at A la Ronde and Peckover, to an entire house at Snowshill, which was filled with objects by wealthy collector and artist Charles Paget Wade (1883–1956).

The original cabinets of curiosities were often social status symbols and conversation pieces designed to showcase influence, knowledge and wealth with objects obtained both through growing international trade and as a result of expanding colonial power. Some cabinets included fabricated objects, such as mermaids and unicorn horns, but from the 18th century onwards there was a growing emphasis on science and the presentation of natural evidence. The collection's organisation and interpretation typically reflected the owner's taste and identity, as well as changing intellectual interests and cultural understanding. Objects from global cultures or representing unfamiliar beliefs – displayed out of context – were frequently included.

'Curiosity' is therefore a word that has many connotations in the history of collecting, and it is used in this book in its broadest sense. In addition to inventions – the products of curiosity – the objects selected have been chosen because they puzzle, intrigue and prompt questions from 21st-century visitors, volunteers and staff at National Trust properties. As well as the significance these objects held for the individuals or families who created, collected, owned or used them, they also offer insights into the social history, tastes, fashions and technologies of their time.

Whether something qualifies as 'curious' is clearly a matter of perspective. A 21st-century mobile phone, driverless car or voice-activated assistant would be curious and astonishing to our ancestors, even if they recognised the purpose of such inventions. Many of the objects in this book that may seem curious to modern eyes because they have an unfamiliar or now obsolete function would not have been considered curiosities when they were first used. Examples include the glass bowl at Townend (pages 152–3) that provided extra light for weavers, and the potsherds at Kingston Lacy that were used by the ancient Egyptians for note-taking (pages 140–1). Both provide insights into the age before electricity provided such marvels as artificial illumination and personal computers. Protective charms such as the witch bottle (page 192), and the microscope used by scientist Mary Ward (1827–69) (pages 190–1) remind us of the enduring belief in magic alongside emerging scientific ideas as people sought to understand their world.

Some objects pique our interest and stir our emotions at the same time, such as the death masks of actors Dame Ellen Terry (1847–1928) and Sir Henry Irving (1838–1905) at Smallhythe (pages 68–9 and right), or the funereal flowers from Queen Victoria for her favourite prime minister (pages 80–1). These immensely personal pieces remind us that objects can hold powerful significance and help preserve memories.

By contrast, some objects were specifically designed to provoke curiosity or amusement, such as the 'tortoise-shell cat' carved into the wall at Knightshayes (page 174), or made of unusual materials and at unexpected scales, such as the extra-long hobby horse at Chastleton (pages 178–9). Objects such as the flintlock tinder lighter at Felbrigg Hall (pages 176–7) or the etui (a small container for personal objects) inside a delicate walnut shell at Coughton Court (pages 100–1) were valued because they were intriguing or novel. Others are accidental creations, rare survivals or ordinary objects that have extraordinary

Above · The gilded plaster death mask of the actor Sir Henry Irving (1838–1905) by Sir George Frampton (1860–1928) in its case at Smallhythe, Kent.

Opposite · The angel of death as a winged skeleton is one of 27 terracotta figures and busts by Victor Alexander Sederbach (active 1755–7) that adorn the walls of Lacock Abbey, Wiltshire (page 175).

connections, such as the pawprint of a dog preserved on a Roman roof tile at Chedworth Roman Villa (pages 20–1) or the bargain birthday gift at Shaw's Corner (page 126) given to George Bernard Shaw (1856–1950). Finally, a few objects show how new technology was used in novel ways, such as the – potentially dangerous – electric jewellery at Cragside (pages 198–9).

The objects in this book are organised into eight broad, overlapping themes, each with a short introduction. These themes explore the function, creation and use of the objects, from toys and labour-saving devices to reminders of love and loss.

While some of the featured objects were created by or purchased new from inventors, manufacturers, artists and designers, others had already had long lives before they came into the National Trust's care. Their history (or provenance) may be harder to trace and, sadly, sometimes the information about who created them or exactly when and where they were acquired, is now lost. Where it is known, this information is included at the end of each entry. A number of the objects were allocated to the National Trust through HM Government's hugely beneficial Acceptance in Lieu of inheritance tax scheme, and this is indicated by the ‡ symbol and the date of acquisition.

This book has been written by eight National Trust curators. Like all good inventions, it builds on existing research and knowledge, in this case from many expert colleagues across the organisation. With over a million objects in the National Trust collections, this book could easily be written many times over and inevitably many intriguing objects have been left out. It should therefore be seen as a starting point for exploring these rich and varied collections. You can discover many more fascinating objects at your leisure through our Collections website (www.nationaltrustcollections.org.uk).

We hope you enjoy this exploration of the unexpected aspects of National Trust collections, and that it inspires you to look with fresh eyes at the innovative and creative objects found in many of the places in our care.

Katie Knowles
Assistant National Curator,
National Trust

Opposite · Detail of a George Bernard Shaw puppet (1949) by Waldo S. Lanchester (1897–1978) at Shaw's Corner, Hertfordshire (page 127).

Overleaf · Part of the 18th-century collection of souvenirs and curiosities displayed in a mahogany secretaire bookcase in the Library at A la Ronde, Devon.

100
CURIOSITIES
&T INVENTIONS

1. HOME COMFORTS

Necessity is the mother of invention, and the following pages feature a remarkable range of innovations that have helped to make homes warmer, safer and more comfortable. Archaeological excavations have revealed that Chedworth Roman Villa in Gloucestershire benefitted from the luxury of underfloor heating, as well as window glass and a tiled roof (even if a Roman dog did leave its pawprints on the drying clay tiles). Time- and labour-saving devices have evolved to improve quality of life and meet basic needs with such innovations as boot dryers and electric hot-water bottles. Other gadgets were designed to protect the home from hazards such as fire, and range from 'extinguisher grenades' to an early insurance plaque. In the realm of transport, the travelling chariot even provided carpeted comfort on the move.

Country-house owners played an important role in the improvement and introduction of many of the home comforts we enjoy today, from central heating and sanitation to artificial illumination. Because properties were often far from urban centres, owners relied on their own sources of power supply. Cragside in Northumberland, for example, was the first private house in the world to be lit by hydroelectricity, using Joseph Swan's newly perfected lightbulbs.

As well as using new technology and ensuring homes were safe, time was spent making spaces welcoming and cosy. Curiosities such as the wooden pet at Snowshill and unusual leather figures at Lytes Cary (one of which is shown opposite) reflect a desire for companionship across the centuries, while personal possessions such as the propped-up pug at Calke Abbey and the innovative electric cup warmer at Castle Drogo give an insight into how people lived and presented their homes.

Pawprint from the past

A Roman dog literally left its imprint on the history of Chedworth Roman Villa. Over 1,600 years ago it walked across this clay tile, preserving its pawprint for posterity. Chedworth was a particularly grand example of a Roman villa, with the luxury of underfloor heating, window glass and a tiled roof. Handmade clay roof tiles were often laid out to dry in the sun before being fired in a kiln, so they were vulnerable to foot- and pawprints.

Dogs had various roles in Roman Britain, including hunting or guarding property and livestock. Some dogs would also have been kept as pets. It is not known what type of dog made this pawprint, but other surviving roof tiles found at Chedworth show prints from deer, pigs and sheep, as well as the impression of a Roman sandal. These marks – frozen in time – reveal something about the environment in which tiles were made, including the domestic and wild animals roaming nearby. The tiles may have been produced in a tile-maker's yard in nearby *Corinium* (Cirencester) or made on-site. KK

Chedworth Roman Villa, Gloucestershire · Tile ·
Clay · 12.5cm (length) · NT 73872.1

Alternative energy

This Chinese cloisonné vase is one of four that were converted to lamps not once but twice, for two different technologies. William, 1st Lord Armstrong (1810–1900), was one of the great scientific innovators of the Victorian age, an immensely successful engineer and armaments manufacturer. He made Cragside a showcase for technology. When the Library was completed in 1872, the vases housed paraffin lamps with the latest Duplex (double) burners, invented in 1865.

Electricity fascinated Armstrong. He attended Joseph Swan's demonstration of his newly perfected incandescent electric lamp in 1879. In December 1880 Swan supervised the installation of his lamps at Cragside – the first house in the world to be lit by hydroelectricity, which was generated on the estate. The copper vase conducted current, and a wire inside dipped through a hole into 'a small, insulated mercury cup' – its contents highly poisonous – in the metal base, which was connected to the power wire. It had no switch: setting the vase onto the base turned it on, removing it turned it off. SP

Cragside, Northumberland · One of a pair of cloisonné vases · *China · Qing dynasty, probably Daoguang period 1821–50, shade c.1880 · Converted to a paraffin lamp c.1872; converted to electricity 1880 · Enamels on copper, glass shade · 45.7cm (height) · NT 1228271.1 · ‡ 1977*

Proof of protection

Before the Great Fire of London in 1666, there was no formal firefighting service and no insurance system to replace lost property. The Great Fire highlighted the need for a more professional arrangement. In 1680, the first modern fire insurance company was established in the City of London. By the early 1700s, other companies had been established and were insuring beyond the City.

The Royal Exchange Assurance of Houses and Goods from Loss by Fire was granted a Royal Charter in 1721. The name and plaque emblem were inspired by the Royal Exchange building where their offices were sited – constructed to replace its predecessor, which had burned down during the Great Fire.

Insured properties displayed the plaques in a prominent position, which helped the companies' retained 'fire men' to identify which building to save. They were installed high up to prevent fraudulent relocations to other properties. The practice died out following the merging of the largest insurance companies in the 1830s, and the development of local fire services over the course of the 19th century. HM

Boar Mill, Corfe, Dorset · Fire insurance plaque · *18th or 19th century* · Lead · *9.3 x 10 x 0.3cm* · NT 420357

The cat's whiskers

Snowshill Manor is a house full to the brim with unusual and special objects. The collection was created by Charles Paget Wade (1883–1956), an architect, artist and craftsman, who inherited his father's sugar estates in St Kitts. The income from these estates allowed him to accumulate a large and varied collection, which he housed in the Manor. Wade himself lived in a small priest's cottage in the courtyard, which was also home to this wooden cat.

The cat was a gift from Wade's friend and fellow collector Professor Albert Richardson (1880–1964). Richardson apparently felt that Wade needed company at Snowshill but didn't think his friend was responsible enough to look after a real pet. Instead, he presented Wade with a life-sized wooden cat. White with black spots, it had realistic whiskers and eyelashes and stood on a rug next to the fire. Despite his friend's doubts, Wade looked after his wooden pet well and, true to his motto 'Let nothing perish', he replaced its whiskers every year. KK

Snowshill Manor, Gloucestershire · Wooden cat · *Wood, paint and hair* · *28 x 64.8cm* · *NT 1332424*

Mystery figures

Two mysterious figures, just over a metre tall, guard the fireplace in the Great Parlour at Lytes Cary (the second appears on page 18). For years they were believed to be rare 17th-century creations because of their Elizabethan costume and hairstyles. The colourful clothing is made from leather embossed with a variety of patterns. While similar moulded leather figures survive in collections across Europe, little is known about their purpose. They were possibly designed as three-dimensional versions of 17th- or 18th-century 'dummy boards', the life-sized painted shapes that created the illusion of a human presence. They may have been used to surprise guests, deter intruders or provide silent companionship.

In 2008, X-ray analysis revealed the presence of a tin can inside the head of one figure, as well as round-headed wire nails. A serrated edge on the can indicates the use of a tin-opener, implying the figures are actually late 19th-century creations. They were probably purchased by Sir Walter Jenner (1860–1948), who bought Lytes Cary in 1907 with the intention of restoring and refurnishing it in an appropriate 17th-century style. KK

Lytes Cary Manor, Somerset · Pair of leather figures · *Late 19th or early 20th century · Leather, wood, varnish and nails · 112 (height) x 40cm (diameter) · NT 254640*

Fire-fighting grenades

'May Heav'n protect our home from flame' begins a prayer in the Servant's Passage at Erddig. Fear of fire was understandable and many country-house owners took precautions, which ranged from sand buckets to fire drills. Patented in 1883 in Chicago, the Harden Star Hand Grenade was invented to help homeowners combat domestic fires. According to contemporary advertisements, these curious blue-ribbed glass bottles were designed to be hurled into a fire. The mixture of water, salt and chemicals inside would boil and produce fumes that could smother the flames.

The grenades were sold by the dozen in the 1880s and there are over 100 grenades dotted around Erddig, purchased by owner Simon Yorke III (1811–94). Erddig suffered several minor fires, all safely extinguished by estate workers but – perhaps fortunately – there is little evidence that these early fire extinguishers were used. Despite glowing testimonials, some were no more effective than sprinkling water on the flames. Later generations of the Yorke family took further precautions against domestic fires, fitting metal ceilings in the property in the early 20th century. KK

Erddig, Wrexham · Harden Star fire extinguisher grenade · *The Harden 'Star' Hand Grenade Fire Extinguisher Co. Ltd* · *Glass · 17cm (height) · NT 1145704*

Feeling the heat

Although it is made in the shape of a hot-water bottle, this bed warmer at Chastleton contains no liquid. The rigid brown case is made from a hard plastic called Bakelite, which was patented in 1909. An asbestos heating tube inside holds an array of wires, which run through the neck of the bottle and can be plugged into a lamp or electric wall socket.

Bakelite was a revolutionary material because it was the first entirely synthetic plastic. Easy to mould into a wide variety of shapes and resistant to heat and electricity, it was used in everything from radios, cars and household items to jewellery. By 1944 over 15,000 different Bakelite products were available. This bed warmer was made by the British company Rothermel, using a patented heating tube insulated by the Bakelite cover. The last private owner of Chastleton, Barbara Clutton-Brock, would have been grateful for a bed warmer like this. She described the house as intensely cold, telling the National Trust when she left that she had never felt warm in her life. KK

Chastleton House, Oxfordshire · Bed warmer · R.A. Rothermel Ltd · 1944–50 · Bakelite, metal · 34 x 19cm · NT 1430403

Travelling in style

For long-distance road journeys, a private carriage was a luxury. Horse-drawn vehicles had provided transport for thousands of years but in the 18th and 19th centuries technological advances and new designs offered greater comfort, speed and privacy for travel on roads that were often rough. Travelling chariots such as this one were well equipped, with cushioned seats, silk roller blinds and carpets. They were pulled by pairs of post-horses, hired at inns along the route.

Chariots enabled leisure travel, such as the European grand tours embarked upon by rich young men, and played a part in international diplomacy. Diplomat Gibbs Crawfurd Antrobus (1793–1861) is believed to have used this chariot. He was Secretary of Legation in Sardinia-Piedmont and to the Two Sicilies in the 1820s, and travelled widely in Europe. This carriage has its original roof-mounted imperials (leather and wood luggage cases) and even a compartment for his dress uniform sword. It has two seats inside; servants rode outside on the rear rumble seat. This is one of the oldest carriages in the National Trust Carriage Museum's collection. KK/SP

Arlington Court and the National Trust Carriage Museum, Devon · Travelling chariot · *B. Clover · c.1815 · Glass, ivory, leather, linoleum, metal, textile, wood · 244 x 193 x 380cm · NT 272895 · Given in 1974*

A nice hot cup of tea

In 1910 entrepreneur and millionaire Julius Drewe (1856–1931) commissioned architect Sir Edwin Lutyens (1869–1944) to design Castle Drogo, the last castle to be built in England. There was nothing medieval about the technology though: Drewe's castle had central heating, numerous bathrooms, a telephone system, a lift and its own electricity supply. The dining table was even fitted with an electric tablecloth, which powered electric candlesticks. Electric tablecloths were among many novelties – some of them potentially lethal – associated with the early years of electricity in the home.

This wonderful brass cup warmer was another of Drewe's gadgets, designed to keep his cup of tea hot. Unlike earlier food warmers, which were powered by fire or candle flame, this device was plugged into one of the castle's 332 electrical sockets and powered by hydroelectricity, generated in the valley below. Drewe had begun work as a tea merchant in China and opened the Willow Pattern Tea Store in Liverpool in 1878. In 1883 he founded the Home and Colonial Stores grocery chain, which specialised in tea from India and was so successful that he was able to retire at the age of 33. KK/SP

Castle Drogo, Devon · Cup warmer · *c.1920–30* · *Brass · 10.2 x 20.3cm · NT 902809*

A silver shoal

This wonderful shoal of fish at Ickworth was collected by Geraldine Anson (1843–1927), 3rd Marchioness of Bristol. Many of the fish are articulated with cleverly arranged rivets, which means they can wiggle from side to side like their real-life equivalents. Most have a hollow compartment inside, designed to hold scent, smelling salts or a sponge soaked in a sweet-smelling oil (known as a vinaigrette). Some incorporate loops so they could be worn on a chain and used as etuis – containers for small objects. Similar articulated fish were sometimes used to contain fragrant spices for the Jewish celebration of Shabbat.

Ickworth in Suffolk is well known for its significant 18th-century silver, collected by the Hervey family. Lady Bristol added these fish to the Ickworth collection in the late 19th century. The original labels show that some were believed to come from Japan, India and Germany, but others include hallmarks for 19th-century Birmingham and London silversmiths. The realistic shapes, scales and fins mean that some of these creatures are even identifiable as pike, flatfish and swordfish. KK

Ickworth, Suffolk · Silver fish · *Various makers* · *19th century* · *Silver* · *Various dimensions* · *NT 852130–852183* · *‡ 1956*

While the iron's hot

Strangely shaped metal objects like this would have been used in the hot and steamy environment of the laundry from the 17th century onwards. While most irons removed creases from clothing, it was also important that ruffles and flounces were not flattened. The goffering iron was developed to keep the curl in frills and the pleats on collars, cuffs and bonnets. The hollow tube of the iron is set horizontally on a stand, allowing a red-hot metal rod or poker to be placed inside. The frills could be curled around the heated tube, like a hair curler. These irons were sometimes known as 'tally' irons, since they were believed to have been introduced from Italy.

This example can be found at Rufford Old Hall, which exhibits five centuries of history. Only the Great Hall survives from the original Tudor structure and the old service wings have been replaced by later extensions, but there was once a laundry and a drying room. Rufford is also home to the Philip Ashcroft collection of household and rural objects, illustrating south-west Lancashire folk life. KK

Rufford Old Hall, Lancashire · Goffering iron · *19th century · Iron and steel · 27 x 37 cm (moulded base 15cm diameter) · NT784156*

Home and dry

These curious foot-shaped metal objects at Dudmaston in Shropshire are boot dryers and airers. The circular brass top was unscrewed, and the dryers filled with hot water. They would then be covered with a thick stocking (to absorb condensation) and slotted inside fishing waders or damp riding boots, slowly drying them from the inside. This pair was owned by Alice Mary Darby (1852–1931), who married into the Wolryche-Whitmore family of Dudmaston.

These boot dryers have the mark of the Army & Navy Stores, a retailer established by army and navy officers concerned by the growing costs of living. By 1900 it had branches in England and India, but until 1922 only subscribing members with army or naval connections were eligible to shop there. Alice's husband, Colonel Francis Wolryche-Whitmore (1845–1927), was in the Shropshire Light Infantry and may well have

qualified. Pairs of these boot dryers, available in either brass or copper, were still being advertised in the company's 1939 catalogue, when they cost up to 35 shillings a pair. KK

Dudmaston, Shropshire · Boot dryers · *Army & Navy Stores Ltd* · *c.1900* · *Tin and brass* · *18.5 x 23.5cm* · *NT 814061*

Propped-up pug

Calke Abbey, nestled in the heart of 18th-century parkland in Derbyshire, is a remarkable survivor from an era of decline. Many country houses were demolished or fell into ruin in the 20th century, as owners struggled to afford the associated running costs and inheritance taxes. In the mid-1950s, an English country house was lost roughly every seven days.

Calke was occupied by the Harpur Crewe family for over 400 years. When the property was transferred to the National Trust in 1985, it was a time capsule in which relatively little had changed since the late 19th century. The Trust carried out essential repairs but decided to preserve the peeling paint, dusty interiors and well-worn family collections to reflect this period of country house decline. This cheeky 19th-century Royal Worcester pug with a broken front leg propped up on a matchbox is an example of the state of 'quiet decay' in which the property is presented. Modelled by George Evans, the pug stands with its tongue out and ears slightly raised, welcoming visitors to this 'unstately home'. KK

Calke Abbey, Derbyshire · Pug · *George Evans (modeller), The Royal Worcester Porcelain Co. Ltd · Modelled 1873 · Porcelain with matt glaze · 40 x 44.5cm · NT 285605 · ‡ 1985*

A jaw-dropping entrance

Victorians loved to showcase natural curiosities, and Cotehele boasts one of the more dramatic displays of this kind. Framing the doorway in the central Great Hall are the jawbones of a fin whale, towering over two metres high. How and why the jawbones of the whale found a home here was a mystery finally solved by researchers at the property in 2016. They were able to connect DNA test results with historical reports of a washed-up sea creature on the shores of Mevagissey Bay.

A note left in an inventory by the 4th Earl of Mount Edgcumbe (1832–1917) reads: 'The jawbones on each side of the centre door are those of a whale (about 61 feet long) landed … January 2nd 1875.' Local newspapers reported this phenomenon, which drew a large crowd to the beach. DNA testing on the bones has since revealed them to be those of a young baleen whale, which, when alive, would have been nearly twice as long as the Great Hall itself. HA

Cotehele, Cornwall · Jawbones of baleen whale · *1875* · *Baleen bone* · *276.5cm (height)* · *NT 348056* · *‡ 1947*

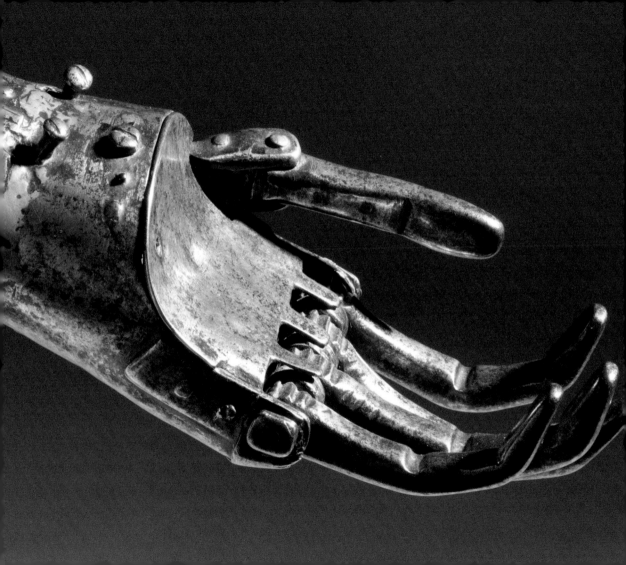

2. HUMAN TOUCH

For hundreds of years in Europe it was believed that the body contained four 'humours', vital bodily fluids that needed to be kept in balance. The objects in this section reflect a changing understanding of the human body over time and advances in the treatment of illness, wounds and disease, such as the moveable prosthetic limbs (similar to the example opposite) invented by pioneering 16th-century surgeon Ambroise Paré.

The 19th century saw many medical advances, including the introduction of anaesthetics (welcomed by Lord Nuffield of Nuffield Place during his appendectomy), protective equipment such as the safety glasses at Souter Lighthouse and the introduction of mass-manufactured medicines that could be kept at home, ready for use, in cabinets like the one at Sunnycroft. However, some early patent remedies, such as the laxatives and poisonous compounds of mercury that were common ingredients in medicines like Chocolate Worm Cakes, could be dangerous to health.

These objects also chart changes in the way people thought about and looked after their bodies. The tongue scraper played its part in the pursuit of the perfect, clean smile and fresh breath in the Georgian period, while the early hairdryer at Wightwick and the portable shower at Erddig show how technology developed to maintain cleanliness and advance self-care. The fashionable beauty spots at Llanerchaeron and the buttonhole box at Anglesey Abbey are small reminders of the desire to keep up appearances.

Safety first

These glasses might look like something out of a dystopian fantasy, but they had a very practical use for the keeper of Souter Lighthouse (below). It is believed that they were worn for protection while cleaning and caring for the lantern room.

But were they designed for the lighthouse keeper, or had they been repurposed from elsewhere? Featuring the same dark lenses and leather side-shields, they are identical to the mountaineering or 'glacier' glasses first used by crystal hunters in the Alps at the end of the 19th century. Pioneered by spectacle-maker Jules Baud, this design prevented mountaineers from going 'snow-blind' by protecting their eyes from the sunlight reflecting off the snow.

Built in 1871 by engineer James Douglass (1826–98), the 22-metre Souter Lighthouse would have been a curiosity in itself, a 'marvel of its age', as the first lighthouse purpose built to be powered by electricity. HA

Souter Lighthouse and The Leas, Tyne and Wear · Safety glasses · *Unknown maker and date* · *Metal, glass, leather* · *2cm (lens diameter)* · *NT 238011.1*

Pioneering prosthetic

This prosthetic arm is a remarkable invention and a survival from a brutal period. Terrible injuries were inflicted on the battlefields of Europe in the 16th and 17th centuries, from arrow and gunshot wounds to the loss of limbs. This led surgeons such as Ambroise Paré (1510–90) to work with armourers to design and produce pioneering prostheses, including mechanically functioning hands and arms. The existing artificial substitutes for amputated limbs, such as wooden pegs, were often stiff and clumsy. Paré wanted them to be more functional, simulating the natural movement of the limb.

This ingenious example has moveable fingers that can be individually locked into place with tiny buttons, allowing a soldier to grip his reins or sword, and giving the wearer some flexibility.

The mechanical arm weighs almost 1.3kg. It is displayed in the Great Hall at Cotehele in Cornwall among examples of weapons and armour, and is known to have been at the property since at least the 1830s. KK

Cotehele, Cornwall · Prosthetic arm · *c.1550–1650* · *Metal · 42cm (length) · NT 347324 · ‡ 1947*

A spoonful of sugar

For centuries cocoa and chocolate have been used to flavour medicines and encourage patients to swallow bitter concoctions. These Chocolate Worm Cakes were advertised by manufacturers Robert Gibson & Sons as a 'delicious Sweetmeat' and were designed to treat intestinal worm infestations. Worm cakes were small, flavoured tablets made

with cinnamon and compounds of poisonous mercury, which destroyed the parasitic worms. Worm infestations were often transmitted by infected food and could be particularly dangerous to the health of malnourished children.

Newspapers and handbills from the 19th and 20th centuries show the huge variety of patent medicines available over the counter. Manufacturers invested large sums to advertise their products to the public. This colourful tin is designed to stand out on the shelf and tempt customers, particularly those unable to afford prescriptions. Doctors' fees could be costly, but these cakes were purchased directly from the chemist for a penny, along with an envelope of instructions. The tin is part of the collection at The Children's Country House Museum, which explores the escapades and challenges of childhood through the centuries. KK

The Children's Country House at Sudbury, Derbyshire
· Chocolate Worm Cakes tin · *Robert Gibson & Sons Ltd* ·
c.1905 · Metal · 14.4 x 15.3cm · NT 662630

A surgical souvenir

Not for the squeamish, this small glass case at Nuffield Place in Oxfordshire has a very personal connection to a former resident. On a specimen slide, covered in preserving fluid, is the appendix of William Morris, 1st Viscount Nuffield (1877–1963), removed by surgery in 1928 and kept on a workbench in his bedroom, among his tools. He had insomnia and would often get up at night to tinker at the workbench.

Lord Nuffield owned the Morris Motor Company and was at one time Britain's richest self-made man, as well as a great philanthropist. He donated substantial sums to the University of Oxford to help establish Nuffield College, and in 1936–7 he also helped to establish Oxford's Postgraduate Medical School. His £2 million donation (the equivalent of around £80 million today) included research endowments for chairs in medicine, surgery and obstetrics, and he offered to fund a fourth chair in anaesthesia. The university was reluctant but Lord Nuffield got his way. His insistence may well have been because of a painful reaction to anaesthetics at the dentist, which contrasted with the pain-free removal of his appendix in 1928. KK

Nuffield Place, Oxfordshire · Human appendix · *1928 · Felt, glass, appendix, preserving fluid, tape, wood · 8.5cm (width) · NT 1651877*

Lotions and potions

Everything in this large medicine cabinet at Sunnycroft in Shropshire is original, including the antiseptic smell. Inside are over 300 medicines and toiletries used by three generations of the Lander family, who lived here until 1997. The contents include bottled remedies, soaps, bandages and packets of pills dating from the 1920s onwards, including many familiar brands and labels.

Until the mid-1800s, many medicines were herbal remedies, but scientific and medical discoveries greatly improved understanding about the human body in the decades that followed. By the 20th century, affordable medicines were readily available over the counter of chemist shops such as Boots (founded in 1849), and were kept in a drawer or cabinet at home ready for use. Unlike earlier patent remedies, these mass-manufactured medicines were subject to rigorous testing.

The Landers' medicine cabinet contains products such as Pepsodent toothpaste, cod-liver oil and Sloan's Liniment for relieving pain associated with rheumatism and arthritis. The liniment's active ingredient is capsicum (chilli pepper), which warms the skin. As well as medicines, the cabinet includes Palmolive shaving cream, Soltan suntan lotion (launched in 1939), and an early solid perfume called Frozoclone. KK

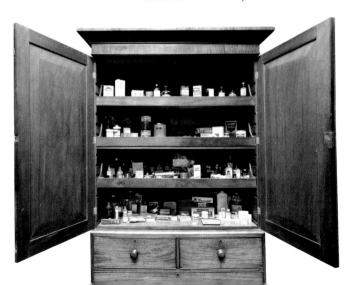

Sunnycroft, Shropshire · Medicine cabinet inside linen press · *Linen press, 1851–75, mahogany, 230 x 129 x 60cm · Various contents, c.1920–97 · NT 1318269*

Beauty spot

A box of *mouches* (literally: 'flies') may sound distasteful to some, but this little box contains a favourite beauty trick of European women for over 200 years. Better known as beauty spots, these small black taffeta pieces were named after their resemblance to a fly that has landed on the wearer's skin.

Popularised by the French in the 18th century and deployed as a cunning way to cover unsightly marks, *mouches* created a map of intrigue across the décolletage. The placement of the beauty spot – on the cheek or by the mouth, for example – also became a coded means of communicating emotions, wealth and even political allegiances.

They were carried in *boites à mouches* (fly boxes). This Maison Dorin box probably dates from around 1880. Somehow, the box ended up in the collection of Pamela Ward (1908–94), owner of both a Knightsbridge antiques shop and a collection of over 5,000 treasures, which she left to the National Trust. The *mouches*, it appears, were as much a curiosity in the early 20th century as they appear to us today. HA

Llanerchaeron, Ceredigion · Paper box containing pieces of black taffeta · *c.1880s* · *Paper, taffeta* · *1.3cm x 3.3cm (diameter)* · *NT 546022*

A hair-raising invention

For thousands of years the options for drying one's hair were limited mainly to using a towel or sitting by a fire. Victorian ingenuity and manufacturing capacity created an explosion of inventions for new products covering every aspect of daily life, including hair and beauty. This item may resemble a weapon, but it is the forerunner of the brush hairdryer, repeatedly brushed through the hair to dry it. It was one of many personal grooming products launched in the late 1800s. In 1890 French stylist Alexander Godefroy invented the first enclosed hairdryer, a bonnet connected to a gas stove.

With silverplate and a decorative handle, this was a relatively expensive model, made by B. Perkins and Son, manufacturers of metal products in the East End of London. There were cheaper ceramic versions. The Science Museum has two stoneware Hincks & Co. 'Thermicon' examples (A650887/2). Their instruction label reads: 'FILL IT WITH BOILING WATER, AND It Dries the Hair after Washing in a few minutes'. It was certainly safer than many early 20th-century electric hairdryers. SP

Wightwick Manor, Wolverhampton · Hairdryer · *Stamped B. Perkins and Son, and SIMPSON PATENTEE · c.1880–1900 · Silverplated brass with ebonised wood handle · 23cm (length) · NT 1288759*

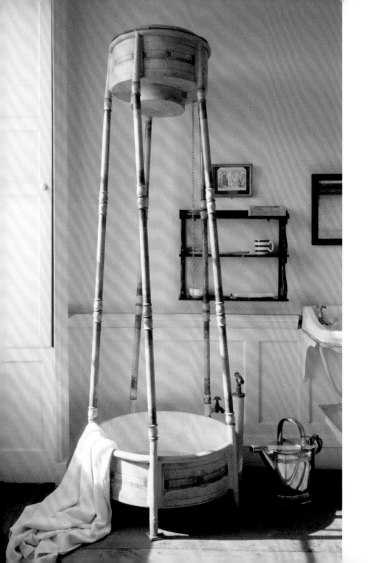

Labour-intensive ablutions

In the first half of the 19th century plumbed bathrooms were uncommon even in grand houses. Servants filled and emptied ewers, basins and hip baths in bedrooms or dressing rooms. Shower baths such as this one were also portable, rather than plumbed in.

A framed copy at Erddig of John Leech's cartoon *Domestic Sanitary Regulations* (opposite), published in the satirical magazine *Punch* in 1850, shows the shower's labour-intensive operation: servants filled the tank at the top with hot water; the water was then released by pulling a chain; finally, the integral stirrup pump was operated to force water from the tray back up the pipes and into the tank to be used again. Leech shows reluctant children wearing oil-cloth conical 'extinguisher caps', which were designed 'to break the fall of the descending torrent upon the head', as American magazine *Godey's Lady's Book* described it in June 1855.

In the 1960s, Erddig's last owner Philip Yorke rigged up a shower with a portable gas ring heating a tank. A suspended rubber hose dribbled out water 'just long enough for a hasty wash'. SP

Erddig, Wrexham · Shower bath · *c.1850* · *Wood, iron and brass, painted to resemble bamboo poles* · *234 x 85cm* · *NT 1147767*

DOMESTIC SANITARY REGULATIONS.

Pursuing the perfect smile

In 1769, famous furniture-maker Thomas Chippendale (1718-79) supplied a bespoke dressing table to Sir Rowland Winn (1739-85), 5th Baronet and owner of Nostell, Yorkshire. Inside the beautifully proportioned table is all that a gentleman would need for daily preparations, including a mirror, cut-throat razors, a shaving brush, pomade pots and this oddly shaped metal gadget – a Georgian tongue scraper.

Tongue scrapers were used to remove 'furry' deposits – food debris, dead cells and bacteria – that could cause bad breath. Tongue scrapers are used in many cultures and metal versions such as this became popular in England in the 18th century. Sugar consumption was rapidly increasing and dental care was unaffordable or inaccessible for many people, so bad breath and rotten or stained teeth were common. Rowland and his wife Sabine (1734-98) took an active interest in medicines and health, and Rowland is known to have experienced gout, chronic headaches and dental problems. Remedies for bad breath and toothache have been found in the Nostell archives, with ingredients including coriander seed, sage and even wine. KK

Nostell, West Yorkshire · Tongue scraper · *Supplied by Thomas Chippendale* · *1769* · *Metal* · *12cm (length)* · *NT 959762.4* · *‡ 1986*

Flower power

Flowers have long been used as fashionable accessories to brighten up outfits. A well-dressed man could often be seen sporting a single flower in the lapel of his suit, and Huttleston Rogers Broughton, 1st Lord Fairhaven (1896–1966), was no exception. Fairhaven, the grandson of an oil magnate, was a keen patron of the arts. He bought Anglesey Abbey in 1926.

Fairhaven was always immaculately dressed, appearing in *Tatler* magazine's list of best-dressed men in 1932. He owned more than 50 suits, which he numbered to ensure he did not wear the same one twice to the same place or occasion. The suits were matched by an elegant *boutonnière*, or buttonhole flower; he wore a coloured carnation for daytime and a white carnation in the evening, which his gardeners grew in the greenhouses. This wooden box with metal cups (left and overleaf), found at Anglesey Abbey, was designed to hold his buttonhole carnations, keeping them fresh and ensuring Fairhaven always looked his best. KK

Anglesey Abbey, Cambridgeshire · Buttonhole box · *1920–60 · Oak and metal · 33 x 83 x 46cm · NT 514667*

Left (above) · Huttleston Rogers Broughton wearing a carnation buttonhole in a portrait by Lafayette Ltd · *Left (below)* · The lid of his buttonhole box.

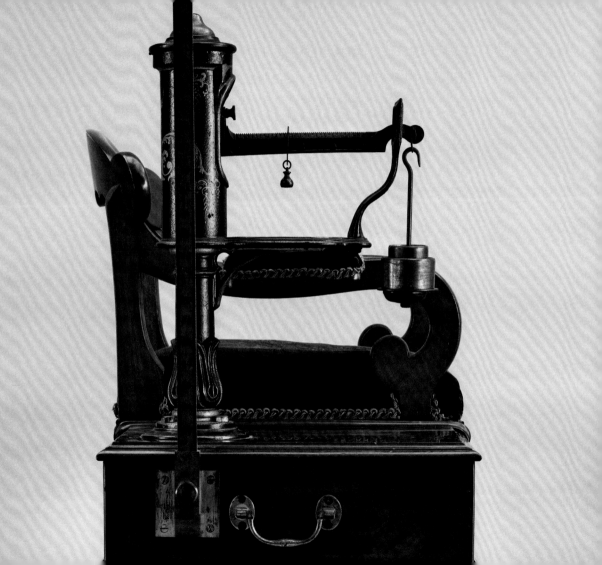

Measuring up

Weighing scales are a common feature in modern homes, used for measuring everything from ingredients to bodyweight. This velvet-padded Victorian seat, which stands in the Oak Staircase at Petworth House, is also a weighing scale. Similar examples could be found in the hallways of country houses or gentlemen's clubs and this one has been recorded at Petworth since at least 1869. It uses a series of brass weights, which can be kept in a drawer under the seat, and also features a measuring pole and carrying handles. These chairs were typically used for weighing jockeys before a race to prevent any rider being lighter than the rest and gaining an unfair advantage. Petworth was certainly home to keen racehorse owners and breeders, including George Wyndham, 3rd Earl of Egremont (1751–1837).

Scales are often associated with managing weight, whether aimed at loss or gain. In a club or country house guests might be weighed at the beginning and end of their visit; a slight weight increase being the sign of good food, a generous host and an appreciative guest. KK

Petworth, West Sussex · Weighing scales · *H.T. Fallows & Co.* · *c.1869* · *Mahogany, textile and metal* · *92.5 x 82 x 47cm; 173cm (height of pole)* · *NT 485362* · *‡ 1956*

3. MEMORY LANE

Objects can hold immense personal significance and act as triggers for memories. Holding a familiar object in our hand and feeling its shape and texture, hearing the sound it makes or smelling its scent, can transport us across time and distance to deeply connect with a moment in the past. This section contains objects that often held particular personal significance in both life and death.

Some of these objects are souvenirs of events, including an English Civil War siege of Corfe Castle and the destruction of an airship. Others, such as the marble sculpture of a foot at Hughenden, hair jewellery and the death mask of a great actress, are immensely personal, preserving physical features and ensuring loved ones are remembered after death. The bunch of dried primroses symbolises a great friendship between a queen and her prime minister, while on the Dodo Terrace at Mount Stewart (opposite) the friends and family of Lady Londonderry are immortalised in stone. The ships, names and dates scratched on the walls at Sissinghurst by French prisoners of war recall a particular period in its history, and the lifelike bronze tortoises at Kingston Lacy are a visible reminder of a collector's fondness for these endearing creatures.

A cosmopolitan tortoise

William John Bankes (1786–1855) was a pioneering Egyptologist and an avid collector of art and antiquities. He was also particularly fond of tortoises, and kept several as pets. While exiled in Europe in October 1853, he commissioned the sculptor Baron Carlo Marochetti (1805–67) to make 16 bronze tortoises to support marble urns he had purchased for the garden of his country estate at Kingston Lacy. With the season of tortoise hibernation imminent, Bankes supplied one of his own pets as the model, and a mould was carefully taken at Marochetti's studio. A letter to his sister reveals his delight at the creature's adventure across Paris for the job.

In addition to having a natural sympathy for this animal, Bankes may have chosen it as a support to allude to the mythological archetype of the 'Cosmic Tortoise', which bears the world on its massive shell. Sharp-eyed visitors to Kingston Lacy will find tortoises elsewhere in its interiors, including six of them as the feet of a pair of candelabra in the Saloon. ARW

Kingston Lacy, Dorset · Set of 16 tortoises · *Cast after the model by Baron Carlo Marochetti, RA · 1853 · Bronze · 7.5 x 15.5 x 21.5cm · Inscribed with Roman numerals · NT 1255562*

Footloose

On a desk in the library at Hughenden sits a marble sculpture of a left foot. Perhaps inspired by the marbles of the classical world so admired by the Victorians, the foot was modelled from Mary Ann Viney-Evans (1792–1872), the wife of former prime minister and prominent statesman Benjamin Disraeli (1804–81). Disraeli's courtship of the wealthy widow – herself something of an unconventional figure – was dismissed by many as fortune-hunting. Their relationship, however, developed into one of mutual respect and love.

Much like death masks, copies of hands or feet helped immortalise or preserve a person's features. These mementos could then be displayed as ornaments or kept as personal keepsakes. We do not know which artist created this piece, but the unusual choice was possibly another tribute to the Greek and Roman sculpture coveted at the time, inspired by the remains of ancient statues on display in institutions such as the British Museum. HA

Hughenden, Buckinghamshire · Sculpture of the left foot of Mary Ann Viney-Evans, 1st Viscountess Beaconsfield · *c.1810–72* · *Marble* · *13.5 x 23.5 x 9cm* · *NT 429107*

Above · Mary Ann Viney-Evans, Viscountess Beaconsfield (1792–1872) in a posthumous portrait of 1872 by James Godsell Middleton (1805–74) at Hughenden, Buckinghamshire (NT 428991).

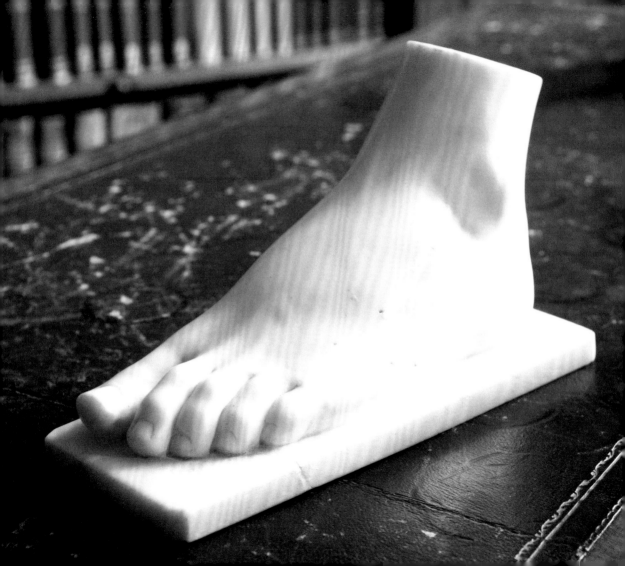

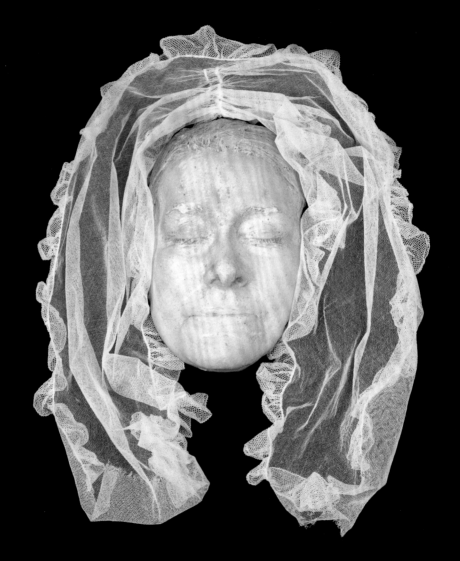

Last act

A jewel of the stage in the late 19th and early 20th centuries, actress Ellen Terry (1847–1928) made her name performing the soliloquies of Shakespeare, taking on the roles of Lady Macbeth, Ophelia and Juliet. Terry bought Smallhythe Place in 1899, and it was here, in 1928, that she died. Journalists from around the UK gathered to report the news, and tributes flooded in from fans across the world.

Death masks may seem macabre, but they were a common way of preserving the likenesses of loved ones after death, a means to ensure they are remembered as in life. For Ellen Terry, this important task was entrusted to Margaret Winser (1868–1944), a local sculptor who had previously exhibited at the Royal Academy. Having spent her life assuming the identity of others on the stage, Terry's final mask reveals only her – peaceful, fragile and as striking in death as she was in life. Her son Edward claimed that, in her final moments, she appeared to be: '…a young beautiful woman [lying] on the bed, like Juliet on her bier'. HA

Smallhythe Place, Kent · Death mask of Dame Ellen Terry · *Margaret Winser* · *1928* · *Plaster* · *24.2 x 15.4 x 8cm* · *NT 1118505*

Above · Ellen Terry (1847–1928) appearing in the role of Beatrice in Shakespeare's *Much Ado About Nothing* performed in 1882 at the Lyceum Theatre, London (NT 1122391).

The keys to the castle

According to family legend, these large metal keys at Kingston Lacy are souvenirs from an English Civil War siege. They are thought to have been given to royalist 'Brave Dame Mary' Bankes (c.1598–1661), who helped defend Corfe Castle (below) from repeated attacks by Parliamentary troops. When the castle finally surrendered in February 1646, the Parliamentarian commander reportedly returned the castle keys to Lady Mary as a gesture of respect for her courage in defending her home. The castle was 'slighted' (deliberately damaged to deny its use to the enemy), and the rubble was reused in local buildings.

Today, historians debate whether Lady Mary was even at the castle when it fell. Records do show, however, that she continued to trace and retrieve family furniture, tapestries and other castle contents that had been stripped, seized and sold. She lived to see the restoration of King Charles II and the return of her family estates. Her proud descendant William John Bankes (1786–1855) commissioned a bronze statue of Lady Mary clutching a key, for the Bankes's new home at Kingston Lacy, thus capturing this important moment in the family's history. KK

Kingston Lacy, Dorset · 31 mounted keys · *c.1500–1625* · *Iron, gilt, wood · Various dimensions · NT 1255200*

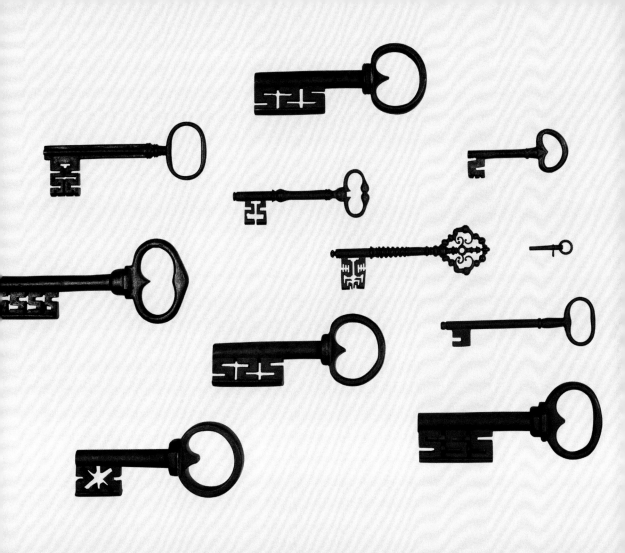

A propaganda coup

This souvenir was crafted from the wreckage of the first German airship brought down in the United Kingdom during the First World War. The conflict was the first total war, in which civilian populations were strategically targeted. Both the British press and public were anxious about raids carried out by German airships – particularly Zeppelins, which the press dubbed 'Baby Killers' in a war of propaganda.

At first, such airships were immune to the limited early air defences, but the introduction of new incendiary bullets helped Lieutenant William Leefe Robinson of 39 Squadron, the Royal Flying Corps, to bring down a German airship on the night of 2/3 September 1916. It crashed in a field behind the Plough Inn at Cuffley, Hertfordshire, killing the entire crew of 16. Lt Robinson was awarded a Victoria Cross, and the press celebrated the victory. The wreckage (opposite) was presented to the British Red Cross Society for the creation of souvenirs, such as this one, which were sold to support its work treating the war wounded. HM

Ickworth, Suffolk · Disc, part of first German airship destroyed over the UK in the First World War · *1916* · *Metal* · *5cm (diameter)* · *Inscribed: 'Part of Zeppelin L.21 Destroyed at Cuffley Sept 2 1916'* · *NT 851604* · ‡ *1956*

Animals at war

This worn wooden post is a reminder of the role animals have played in warfare. It was used by the Hon. Sir Percy Herbert (1822–76) to tether his horse during the Crimean War (1853–6). Herbert was the second son of the 2nd Earl of Powis and served as Quartermaster General (in charge of supplies) during this major European conflict.

Horses were used by the British Army for transporting supplies, equipment and artillery pieces, as well as by the cavalry. With limited shelter available, soldiers tied up their horses in the open with ropes attached to picket posts, which were hammered into the ground. Tragically, many of the horses and soldiers starved or died of cold or disease before they even reached the battlefield.

Herbert was wounded twice during the campaign and when he returned home to Powis Castle in 1856 he received a rapturous public reception. His picket post is displayed at the castle with his medals and swords. Herbert's horse, Inkerman, also returned to Wales, and is buried in the grounds of the Powis estate. KK

Powis Castle and Garden, Powys · Picket post · 1854–5 · *Wood and metal · 69cm (length) · Inscribed: 'COLONEL HONBLE PERCY HERBERTS PICKET POST CRIMEA 1854–5' · NT 1180891.1 · ‡ 1963*

Above · Portrait of the Hon. Sir Percy Herbert (1822–76) with a tented encampment in the background, *c*.1857, by Sir Francis Grant PRA (1803–78) at Powis Castle, Powys (NT 1180924).

A model pet

Children's author and farmer Beatrix Potter (1866-1943) is best known today for her tales of beloved characters such as Peter Rabbit, Jemima Puddle-Duck and Mrs Tiggy-Winkle. These anthropomorphic creatures found a home in the dramatic landscapes of the Lake District, while their likenesses often came from the menagerie of pets kept by Potter in her family home.

Benjamin Bouncer, or 'Bounce', was purchased by Potter from a shop in Uxbridge around 1880. A tame Belgian Hare (a breed of domestic rabbit), Benjamin became her loyal companion, both at home, where he would beg for buttered toast at the sound of the tea bell, and on summer holidays. He became Potter's model for her first foray into publishing when she produced a range of Christmas cards.

Benjamin died in 1892 and this is thought to be his pelt, preserved by Potter – who was a skilled naturalist, accustomed to maintaining the skeletons of deceased pets – to aid the accuracy of her drawings. Benjamin was further immortalised in *The Tale of Benjamin Bunny* in 1904. HA

Hill Top and Beatrix Potter Gallery, Cumbria · Rabbit's pelt · *c.1892* · *Fur* · *57.5 x 35cm* · *NT 642290*

Right · A framed photograph of Benjamin Bunny taken by Beatrix Potter (and inscribed by her) between 1880 and 1892, now at the Beatrix Potter Gallery, Cumbria (NT 242373).

A token of love and luxury

Lady Katherine Charteris Wemyss (1801-44) is believed to have presented this charming piece of jewellery to her husband, George Harry, Lord Grey of Groby (1802-35), to mark the occasion of their marriage. The gold locket is engraved on the reverse with her married initials and the date of the wedding. Inside is a delicate yet vivid depiction of Katherine, likely to be the work of successful portrait miniaturist Sir William Charles Ross (1794-1860).

The construction of the broad strap is poignant. At first glance it could easily be mistaken for fabric, but closer inspection reveals it to be plaited hair sewn onto a velvet lining for comfort against the skin. The personal sentiment of this object suggests it contains hair

from Katherine's own ringlets, similar in colour to further examples of hair-work at Dunham Massey. Hair-work was extremely popular in the Georgian era, and not solely reserved for mourning and remembrance. EC

Dunham Massey, Cheshire · Plaited hair bracelet, set with gold miniature of Katherine Charteris Wemyss, Lady Grey of Groby · *c.1824* · *Hair, gold, metalwork, paint* · *19.1 x 4.6cm* · *Engraved 'KG of G Dec 20th 1824'* · *NT 936127*

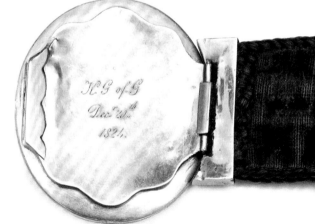

Poignant primroses

This dried spray of primroses with handwritten labels is a symbol of a bond between prime minister and queen. On 26 April 1881, mourners gathered at Hughenden to witness the quiet funeral of former prime minister Benjamin Disraeli, 1st Earl of Beaconsfield (1804–81). Among the tributes received in the following days was a wreath of fresh primroses given in 'affectionate remembrance from Victoria R'. Since Disraeli's first premiership in 1868, Queen Victoria (1819–1901) had sent him bunches of spring blooms, and poignantly chose what she believed to be his favourite flowers for the funeral wreath.

Soon afterwards the humble primrose began to take on a more political significance, as Disraeli – who had often divided opinion in life – became a posthumous Conservative icon. In 1883 the Primrose League was founded to promote Conservative values and generate support for the Conservative Party. By 1891 this popular political movement had over one million members. They wore primrose badges and marked 'Primrose Day' on 19 April – the anniversary of Disraeli's death – by laying wreaths on his grave and around his statues, like this one (opposite) at Parliament Square, London, in 1900. KK

Hughenden, Buckinghamshire · *Dried primroses* · *1881* · *Paper, primroses, string* · *19cm (length)* · *NT 428886*

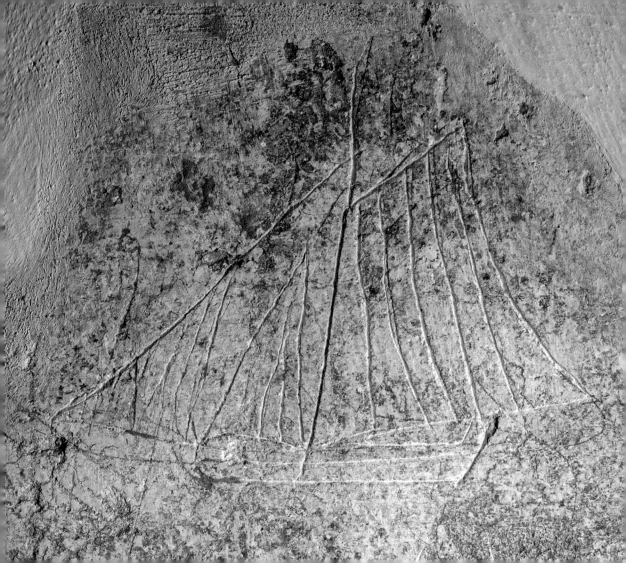

The art of war

Graffiti depicting a ship in full sail was scratched into the wall of the tower at Sissinghurst sometime during the Seven Years War (1756–63). This violent power struggle between France and nations across Europe and the globe saw many men captured and imprisoned. It is believed that up to 3,000 French prisoners were incarcerated at Sissinghurst, some of whom literally left their mark on its history.

As well as ships, names and dates were found etched into the soft stone during conservation work in 2018, a tangible link to the men held here against their will. Little is known about the individuals who created these graffiti, but the tower generally housed French naval officers. Overcrowding and brutal punishments meant that Sissinghurst was considered one of the worst military prisons in the country. A painting from the time, thought to be by an inmate, shows red-coated English guards attacking the prisoners. Letters written by the imprisoned seamen to their families described the prison as 'Chateau de Sissinghurst', one reason the house is known today as Sissinghurst Castle. KK

Sissinghurst Castle Garden, Kent · Graffiti · *French prisoners of war* · *1750–60s* · *NT 803649*

Animal alter egos

Four plump dodos, cast in concrete, preside over the Italianate Garden at Mount Stewart. Animals extant and extinct surround them, including a cheetah and a dinosaur lounging amid lush and fragrant planting.

Conceived by Edith, Lady Londonderry (1878–1959), the Dodo Terrace was laid out after the First World War, when she and her husband Charles, 7th Marquess of Londonderry (1878–1949), a serving officer, had opened their London home as the 'Ark', a retreat for friends involved in the war effort. Edith gave each member a pseudonym – animal or mythical – and later immortalised them in idiosyncratically playful garden statuary at Mount Stewart. Charles was 'Charley the Cheetah', while

Edith's father, Henry, 1st Viscount Chaplin MP (1840–1923), evoked the dodo in his old-school manner. Daddy the Dodo, Edith remarked, was 'representative of an elder England', of a 'type of landed gentry' soon to become obsolete, like the bird.

The creatures were modelled by a local sculptor, Thomas Beattie (c.1866–1948), and are arranged around his sculpture of Noah's Ark (see page 62), a symbol of the haven Edith created in the midst of war. ARW

Mount Stewart, County Down · Four dodos · *Thomas Beattie · 1920s · Concrete · 64 x 41 x 64cm · NT 1221067.1-4*

A cherished 'hair-loom'

Robert Devereux, 2nd Earl of Essex, KG (1565–1601), was a favourite of Elizabeth I (1533–1603), until he mounted an abortive coup against the queen and was executed for treason. By repute, these earrings are made with locks of hair cut from his head before his death on the scaffold in 1601. The use of hair in commemorative jewellery, also associated with the death of other public figures such as Charles I (1600–49), created intimate mementos of the deceased.

These earrings belonged to Essex's daughter Frances, Duchess of Somerset (1599–1674). A portrait of Frances by Flemish Baroque artist Sir Anthony van Dyck (1599–1641) (private collection) depicts her wearing a hair earring, possibly one of these. The earrings were passed down the female line to her three-times great-granddaughter, Grace Carteret, Countess of Dysart (1713–55). Carteret brought the earrings

to Ham House on her marriage to the 4th Earl of Dysart, Lionel Tollemache (1708–70) in 1729, and placed them in the Green Closet among her new family's most prized treasures. HM

Ham House, Surrey · Hair earrings · c.1600 · Human hair, enamel, metal · 6 x 0.8cm and 9.5 x 0.8cm · NT 1140215.1 and NT 1140215.2 · Acquired by HM Government in 1948 and transferred to the Victoria and Albert Museum; transferred to the National Trust in 2002

Dying to be reminded

The term memento mori – Latin for 'remember you must die' – describes items that used imagery such as skulls, timepieces or wilting flowers in art and architecture to remind observers of their mortality and the inevitability of death. The idea had its roots in classical antiquity but increased in popularity from the 17th century onwards.

This oak, coffin-shaped box was given to Llanerchaeron by Pamela Ward (1908–94), an antiques collector and dealer. It opens via a hinged pin to reveal the interior compartment, and would have been used to hold snuff (finely ground tobacco leaves). The practice of taking snuff became popular in Europe in the 16th and 17th centuries. By the 18th century its harmful effects were beginning to be realised, but snuff nevertheless remained popular throughout the 19th century. The coffin shape draws on the imagery of memento mori, and may have been a tongue-in-cheek reminder of the perils of snuff use. Other similar examples even feature a second drawer containing a tiny skeleton. HM

Llanerchaeron, Ceredigion · Snuffbox in the form of a coffin · *19th century · Mahogany, oak and metal · 3.2 x 3.6 x 8.9cm · NT 549451*

4. CAPTURING CREATIVITY

Many of the curious objects in this book showcase the craft of their makers. Objects made in miniature, from a mining diorama in a bottle to a delicate walnut container, contrast with a series of grand dragon heads on the lawn at Wallington. Some of the creations reflect popular art forms of their time, such as the shell-craft with which the Parminter cousins lovingly decorated the walls of their home, A la Ronde, or a revival of historical techniques, such as the modern sampler worked into the design of a computer display at Montacute. Many, like the bone inlay picture at Chirk (opposite), are intricate works of art.

Images of nature, people, places and objects are captured here using different techniques and materials, including wax portraiture, ground and polished semi-precious stones, and even taxidermy. A fore-edge painting delicately conceals a picture on the edges of the pages of a book at Tyntesfield, while images of lace and leaves on paper at Lacock are a product of early photography. A rare fragment of beautifully coloured Roman glass serves as a reminder of the spread of techniques and designs through travel and trade, while a homemade doorbell at Snowshill shows the ingenious craftmanship of a former resident.

A gallery from the sea shore

Pursuing artistic practices was common for 18th-century women of the upper classes, but unmarried cousins Jane Parminter (1750–1811) and Mary Parminter (1767–1849) took their work beyond the canvas. Instead, they used the walls of A la Ronde, their 16-sided house in Exmouth (below).

Shell-craft was a popular art form and the Parminters experimented with it throughout A la Ronde. Most spectacularly, an entire shell gallery (overleaf) was created at the top of the house, its walls adorned with natural and decorative curiosities, including sand, ceramic fragments, moss, lichen and bone. The materials were secured onto pieces of card before being plastered into fantastical patterns. Watercolours of birds and botanicals completed the intricate design of the gallery, alongside a painting of a crown.

The gallery's delicate features and the narrow staircase mean that it is no longer accessible, but visitors seeking a glimpse of the shell gallery can do so via a virtual tour. HA

A la Ronde, Devon · Shell gallery · *1796–1849* · *Plaster, shells, bone, ceramics, paint, lichen, sand*

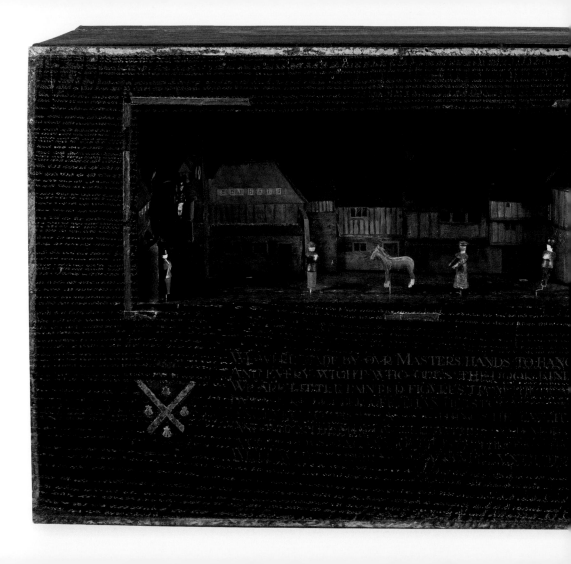

WE WERE MADE BY OUR MASTERS HANDS TO HANG
AND EVERY WIGHT WHO GIVES THE BOOK KIND
WE ARE LITTLE PAINTED FIGURES HOW

Mechanical marvel

Charles Paget Wade (1883–1956) filled Snowshill Manor in Gloucestershire with remarkable objects from around the world, often collected from local antiques dealers, but also things he had made himself. His skill as an artist and craftsman is clear from thousands of surviving sketches, paintings and objects, including this wonderful, mechanised doorbell, which would have been mounted above a door.

Inside the small, rectangular cabinet is the scene of a European marketplace. When a visitor opened the door, this would power the mechanism and set in motion a music box and tiny figures. A canvas belt helped the figures, including toy soldiers and horses, move across the market square. Conservation work has revealed a secret door in the side of the case, with a window and tiny net curtain. A verse painted on the case reveals that Wade made the piece in December 1914, around five years before he purchased Snowshill. The playful doorbell reflects Wade's love of provoking wonder and surprise among his visitors. KK

Snowshill Manor, Gloucestershire · Doorbell · *Charles Paget Wade* · *1914* · *Wood, metal, paint* · *20 x 20 x 33cm* · *NT 1339351*

Here be dragons

Four striking dragons' heads lie on the lawn at Wallington in Northumberland. These magnificent carved stone sculptures are believed to be part of a group that once adorned Bishopsgate, proudly guarding an entrance to the City of London. The historical gate was rebuilt in the 1730s, but just 30 years later it had become too small for London's growing traffic. The dragons were removed and the gate was demolished in the 1760s, along with other City of London gates including Ludgate, Cripplegate and Aldgate.

The dragons were purchased as architectural salvage by the owner of the Wallington estate, Sir Walter Calverley Blackett (1707–77), 2nd Baronet. Along with other pieces of sculpture, he allegedly used the dragons as ballast on his coal barge up the coast to Newcastle. It is thought that he displayed the impressive heads for a time at the Gothic folly Rothley Castle, built in around 1755 on the hillside above Wallington. Since 1928 they have watched over visitors from their current position on the lawn. KK

Wallington, Northumberland · Stone dragon heads · *Christopher Horsnaile the Elder (c.1658–1742)* · *1733/4* · *Limestone* · *71.1 x 104.1cm* · *NT 584972*

Right · Demolished in the 1760s, the appearance of Bishopsgate, surmounted by sculptures of winged dragons, is recorded in Walter Harrison's *History of London*, published in 1775.

A curious call to arms

Animal-inspired instruments have existed for thousands of years, and include the snake- and dragon-head 'zoomorphic' bells used by the Celts and the Romans. This colourful instrument – known as a *buccin à tête de dragon* – was bought by collector Charles Paget Wade (1883–1956). He admired the craftsmanship of the dragon and believed it might be Burmese in origin, although it was actually created for 19th-century French and Belgian military bands.

Buccin or dragon-bell trombones were usually made from a sheet of brass hammered over a wooden form and painted in bright gold, red and green. Some even had a flapping metal tongue, which moved when the instrument was played. Sadly, this *buccin* is missing its mouthpiece and trombone slide, but it would have been an impressive and intimidating sight as the band marched along. There are over 100 complete musical instruments from across the globe at Snowshill, as well as an assortment of detached parts, and it is easy to see why this dragon's head appealed to Wade. KK

Snowshill Manor, Gloucestershire · Buccin · *c.1800–30 · Brass · 65 x 44cm · NT 1335326*

'Nut' what you expect

This walnut at Coughton Court, collected by a member of the Throckmorton family, holds some curious contents. Nestled neatly inside the nutshell are two small bottles for scent, two pairs of scissors and a needle-case. This tiny treasure, with its mounted metal hinges, is an etui or *nécessaire*, a small ornamental case fitted with implements for daily use. Etuis were popular in Europe from the 17th to the 19th centuries and contained a range of miniature contents, including needlework tools, cosmetics and ivory writing tablets.

Large walnut shells made ideal novelty containers for transporting small trinkets or jewellery. Another example, in the collection at Snowshill in Gloucestershire, once held a pair of fine Limerick gloves. A number of walnut-shell etuis survive from the 18th and 19th centuries, when they were sold as elegant gifts and love-tokens in Paris. The size and delicacy of the sewing tools inside meant they were best suited to fine needlework, such as embroidery. Interestingly, crushed walnut shells are sometimes used in pin cushions to keep needles clean and sharp. KK

Coughton Court, Warwickshire · Etui · *Probably 19th century* · *Walnut shell, metal, glass* · *4.5 x 3.5cm* · *NT 135763.1* · *Purchased by private treaty in 2004*

The work in this box is mended by me Mathew Buchinger, born without hands or feet in Germany June 3, 16...

Small world

This remarkable glass bottle contains a busy scene. Tiny wooden figures wield tools and operate miniature mining machinery across two levels. A label on one side of the bottle reads 'After October the 20 1719. This work in this bottle is mendet by me, Matthew Buchinger, born without hands or feet in Germany June the 3 1674.'

The construction of objects or dioramas inside glass bottles became popular in Europe in the late 17th and early 18th centuries. Some of the earliest surviving bottles featured people, tools and mining scenes such as this one, which was collected by Charles Paget Wade (1883–1956). Later bottles featured religious symbols, tokens of faith and miniature ships. Matthew Buchinger (1674–1740), whose name appears on the bottle, was a German artist, magician and calligrapher. He gained particular fame for his dexterity, which he demonstrated in public performances, and for his micrography (illustrations consisting of very small text). This 'whimsy bottle' at Snowshill is an impressive creation and shows a great deal of skill. KK

Snowshill Manor, Gloucestershire · Bottle · *Matthew Buchinger · 'mendet' 1719 · Glass, wood, metal, wax, paper · 22 x 11 x 11cm · NT 1333094.1*

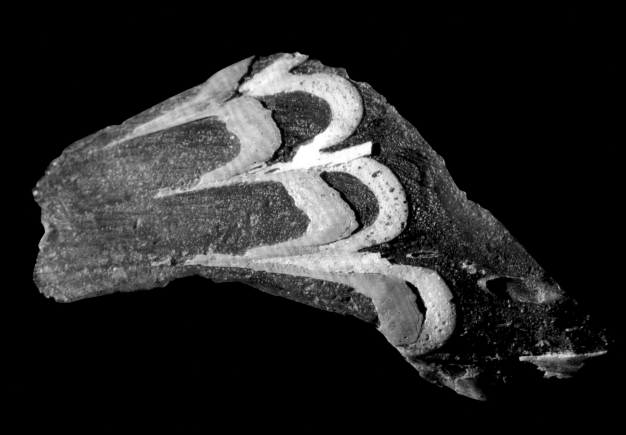

A fishy find

This fragment of patterned Roman glass was found during an archaeological dig in 2017 at Chedworth in Gloucestershire. Chedworth is one of the largest and finest examples of a Roman villa in Britain and by AD 370 it had become a place of luxury. Its rich decoration and fine mosaics demonstrate the wealth and influence of those who lived there, as does this small piece of glass. It is believed to have been imported from the Black Sea and is an extremely rare find.

After studying the scale pattern and looking at other surviving examples of Roman glass, experts were able to identify the piece as a fragment from the 'tail' of a fish-shaped bottle (like the one shown in the artist's impression below). The fish's mouth would have formed the bottle opening and it may have contained perfume or ointment. The scales were created in loops of yellow and white, contrasting with the blue-green glass. Its journey 1,800 years ago from the far regions of the Roman Empire to a villa in rural Gloucestershire is a reminder that there is much more still to learn about Roman life in Britain. KK

Chedworth Roman Villa, Gloucestershire · Glass fragment · *Coloured glass* · *Probably 2nd century AD* · *NT 72374*

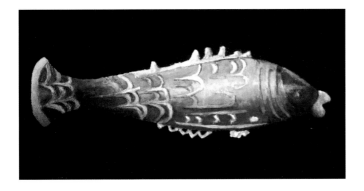

What a relief

Emerging from the background in high relief, these miniature portraits of a man and a woman seem, rather uncannily, to inhabit their frames. They are modelled in coloured wax in lifelike detail, their bodies swathed in swags of silk and velvet to enhance the illusion. Made in the late 18th or early 19th century, the sitters are unidentified, but the style of their dress and hairdos, particularly the man's wig, dates from around 1720, suggesting that the portraits may have been made from images rather than from life.

Wax was a favoured medium for anatomical models, sculptural reliefs and portrait miniatures. It was inexpensive, easy to mould and could be used to model finely detailed forms. Polychrome wax likenesses were particularly popular from the late 18th century among middle and upper classes alike, and several women artists had successful careers as wax portraitists. An example by the popular wax sculptor Samuel Percy (1750–1820) survives at The Argory, County Armagh (NT 564569), with an inscription suggesting that the portrait should be viewed parallel to a window so that the subject's features are enhanced 'by Light and Shadow'. ARW

Treasurer's House, York · Portraits of a man and woman · *British (English) School · c.1800 · Polychrome wax, fabric, in oval wood frame · Both portraits 30.5 x 26cm · NT 592790.1–2*

Chasing shadows

It was at his home, Lacock Abbey, that pioneer photographer William Henry Fox Talbot (1800–77) conducted his early experiments. His interest in capturing images on paper was partly driven by his frustration in sketching the scenery on holiday in 1833. He called his early paper negatives 'photogenic drawings' because they were produced by light. Talbot placed leaves or lace on the surface of a paper coated in salt solution and silver nitrate (which grows dark in sunlight). When exposed to the sun, a delicate impression of the object appeared on the paper. More salt solution stabilised the shadowy picture and created a paper negative. Photogenic drawing was too slow to practically capture pictures of people, but these experiments contributed to the discovery of the negative-to-positive process. In 1835 Talbot created the world's earliest negative (a view of the Latticed Window at Lacock). His negatives could be reproduced multiple times, paving the way for modern photography. Most of Fox Talbot's original negatives are now kept in various museum collections around the world. Visitors to the Fox Talbot Museum can still see reprints of original images like this one. KK

Lacock Abbey and Fox Talbot Museum, Wiltshire ·
A Piece of Lace (reprint) · *William Henry Fox Talbot* ·
Copy print c.1989 · Paper · 22.8 x 18.6cm · NT 1113896

Above · William Henry Fox Talbot (1800–77) photographed at Lacock Abbey, Wiltshire, by John Moffat of Edinburgh, *c.*1865.

Hidden talents

This striking piece of folk art, with its border of oak leaves, shows a view of Chirk Castle in Wrexham. It was presented to the Myddleton family at Chirk by William Roberts (c.1801–78), the porter at Ruthin Castle in Denbighshire, another family property. The unusual picture was made by inlaying ebonised oak with delicate slivers of bone, and is modelled on an engraving from 1735, showing Chirk's magnificent wrought-iron gates in their original position.

Relatively little is known about Roberts, although census records reveal he was a gentleman's servant before he became castle porter. He was clearly a skilled craftsman, and his other known works include inlaid tables and pairs of fire screens depicting Welsh properties, one of which survives at Charlecote Park in Warwickshire (NT 532997). Roberts gave this personalised picture to Fanny Mostyn Owen (c.1810–87), wife of Colonel Robert Myddelton Biddulph (1805–72), in 1861. It is still displayed in the Gothic Revival Cromwell Hall at Chirk today. KK

Chirk Castle, Wrexham · Bone inlay picture · *W. Roberts* · 1858 · *Ebonised oak and bone* · 101.5 x 94.5 x 5.5cm · *Inscribed on reverse: 'Done by W. Roberts the porter, presented to Mrs R M Biddulph Chirk Castle by W. Roberts 1861'* · NT 1171011 · ‡ 1999

Fit for a king

Originally from South America, pineapples were first introduced to Europe and successfully cultivated by the Dutch in the 17th century. Due to the enormous cost of import and cultivation, they became an elite commodity that represented wealth and colonial success. Pineapples were often bought – or even rented – as table centrepieces, to be admired but not eaten.

Due to their crown-like foliage, pineapples became associated with royalty and were beloved of rulers including Louis XV of France (1710–74) and Charles II (1630–85), who even commissioned a portrait of himself being presented with a pineapple.

This jewelled pineapple was owned by Baron Ferdinand de Rothschild (1839–98), and was probably made in the mid-18th century in France. The gilt-bronze dolphins may allude to the maritime strength that enabled the fruit to be brought to Europe, or to the French royal heir, the Dauphin. The botanical accuracy and tiny rock-crystal bee suggest that the maker had a keen interest in the natural world. HM

Waddesdon Manor, Buckinghamshire · Ornamental pineapple · *c.1740–60 · Garnet, semi-precious stone, spinel, serpentine marble, jade, rock crystal and gilt bronze · 24.1 x 19.6 x 18.4cm · Waddesdon 2684 · Bequeathed by James de Rothschild, 1957*

Sporting squirrels

Two opponents eye one another cautiously as they sportingly shake hands and prepare for a boxing match. The fight takes place across five cases at Castle Ward, but these competitors are no ordinary boxers. Created by Victorian taxidermist Edward Hart (1847–1928), this tableau, called 'The Prize Fight', features boxing red squirrels. The set would originally have consisted of six scenes, with each squirrel wearing a coloured sash and boxing gloves. The fight plays out until the victorious, red-sashed squirrel stands over its vanquished opponent.

We might find this distasteful today, especially because native red squirrels are in decline in the United Kingdom. The Victorians, however, were intrigued by this anthropomorphic taxidermy, setting up stuffed animals in poses as if they were miniature humans. Squirrels and frogs were often used, since their shapes and body proportions were well suited to imitating humans. Red squirrels were frequently shot by local foresters protecting their trees, but numbers have fallen dramatically since the 19th-century introduction of grey squirrels from North America. Taxidermy specimens like these were prized by collectors for study as well as dramatic display. Today the Trust works with conservation partners to monitor and protect red squirrel populations in England, Wales and Northern Ireland. KK

Castle Ward, County Down · Tableau of boxing squirrels · *Edward Hart · c.1900 · Taxidermy, glass, wood · 38.7 x 48.2 x 17.8cm · NT 836091.1–5 · Purchased in 1967 with a grant from the Ulster Land Fund*

Now you see it, now you don't

The pages of this copy of Sir Walter Scott's *The Lady of the Lake*, shelved in the magnificent Victorian Gothic Revival library at Tyntesfield, hold a secret. On the fore edge, beneath a patina of shimmering gilt, is a picture that only reveals itself when the pages are fanned. When the book is closed, the image disappears.

Applied in watercolour, this 'vanishing' view of Warwick Castle was adapted from contemporary topographical prints and was probably painted by an artist working for the London publishers Taylor & Hessey (active 1806–25). The book was placed in a vice with its pages fanned to form an inclined fore edge, the image was then painted onto the surface and gilded.

Readers may note that Warwick Castle does not appear in Scott's poem, which is set in the Scottish Highlands. While it was not unusual for fore-edge paintings to depict different subjects from the books they embellished, here the painter clearly intended to evoke the romantic associations inherent in both. ARW

Tyntesfield, North Somerset · Fore-edge painting of Warwick Castle · *Unknown, probably contemporary artist, bound by Taylor & Hessey · After 1810 · Watercolour under gilt · fore edge (unfanned) 2.5 x 20.8cm; book 13.5 x 22 x 3cm · NT 3109455*

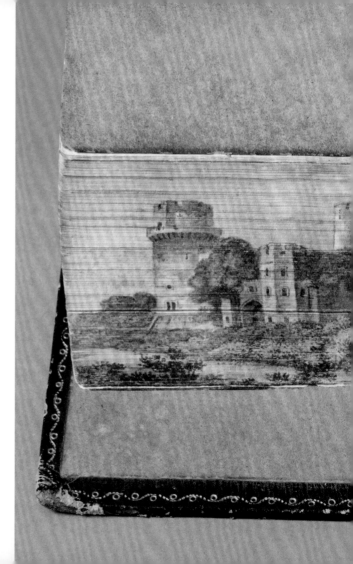

Something old, something new

When Montacute House came to the National Trust in 1931, it was virtually empty. Many of its current furnishings are gifts from supporters, including Dr Douglas Goodhart. In 1988 he donated a group of 130 samplers dating from the early 17th to the 20th centuries, a collection of international importance.

Samplers were originally practical pieces, used by experienced embroiderers to record and practise the patterns and stitches for more significant items, such as clothing and furnishings. Later, samplers became educational tools, with rows of numbers or letters to teach new needlework skills. Some (like the example shown below) featured the names and dates of the young women and children who embroidered them.

This witty modern example in the Goodhart collection – entitled 'Peace' – was made by artist Joan Syrett in April 1984. Like many early samplers, it contains rows of letters, but these are cleverly set out like a computer keyboard instead of alphabetically. The final letters are the artist's initials, J.S., and the sampler demonstrates a range of stitches to form a picture of a computer circuit board and display. KK

Montacute House, Somerset · Sampler · *Joan Syrett (active 1984)* · *1984* · *Textile* · *52 x 42cm* · *NT 597769* · *Gift from Dr Goodhart*

Left · An early needlework sampler in the Goodhart collection at Montacute House, Somerset. Embroidered by Mary Postle in 1747, the design includes rows of letters and numerals, verses and flowers (NT 597735).

5. CLAIM TO FAME

While the cult of celebrity might seem a modern phenomenon, our ancestors were equally intrigued by stories of famous (and infamous) people. The National Trust looks after the homes and collections of many celebrated historical figures, some of whom are represented here through objects they owned, used and treasured.

Objects can be prized for their associations – real or imagined – with celebrated figures. In the National Trust collections these include the garters at Snowshill that are believed to have belonged to the controversial French queen Marie Antoinette, and the humble pencil sharpener given to writer George Bernard Shaw. Some were made especially for a famous

individual, such as the golden winkle at Chartwell presented to Sir Winston Churchill, or were used in the work of celebrated authors and artists. Objects such as the signed fan presented to Prime Minister Benjamin Disraeli by his fellow diplomats and the marionette puppet of George Bernard Shaw reflect the admiration and respect in which they were held during their lifetimes.

While some of these pieces, such as the panda at Chartwell (opposite), belonged to internationally celebrated individuals, others have more modest claims to fame. This section therefore also includes a figurehead given to a local hero who saved lives at sea, a manufacturing marvel and a natural curiosity that became a famous 19th-century visitor attraction.

The gambler's coat

This coat was a manufacturing marvel of its time. From the late 1700s, the textile industry experienced a technological revolution, with new inventions and machinery speeding up cloth production. In 1811 mill-owner John Coxeter of Newbury allegedly boasted of the efficiency of his new mill machinery. Sir John Throckmorton, 5th Baronet (1754–1819), made a 1,000-guinea bet, challenging Coxeter to make a coat in one day. Coxeter had from sunrise, when the wool was on the backs of two sheep, to sunset, when the finished coat would be worn to dinner.

At 5am on 25 June 1811 the sheep-shearing began. The wool was washed, spun into yarn, spooled, warped, loomed and woven into cloth. Local tailors cut, stitched and sewed it, and the finished coat was completed in just over 13 hours. Thousands of people reportedly gathered to watch Coxeter win his bet, and celebrated with beer and roasted mutton when he did. The coat – and an oil painting commemorating the achievement, displayed at the Great Exhibition in 1851 – can still be seen at Sir John's home, Coughton Court. KK

Coughton Court, Warwickshire · Coat · *John Coxeter and Isaac White · 25 June 1811 · Wool · 105 x 53 x 28cm · NT 135713 · Purchased by private treaty with the help of the National Heritage Memorial Fund in 1991/2*

Support act

This pair of exquisitely embroidered garters at Snowshill Manor is said to have belonged to the last *ancien régime* queen of France. Beribboned garters – bands worn around the leg to keep up stockings – were made in the late 18th century before the introduction of elastic. This pair includes tiny coiled springs inside the silk, a fastening patented in 1783 by inventor Martin van Butchell (1735-1814), who also designed springs for artificial teeth.

A woman's garter was a personal and symbolic accessory, associated with the ritual of toilette (getting ready for the day) but also with flirtatious behaviour. These hand-stitched garters were probably purchased by Charles Paget Wade (1883-1956) at auction for his important historical textile collection.

Although difficult to prove, the suggestion that these intimate items of clothing belonged to the controversial, fashion-conscious French queen Marie Antoinette (1755-93) added to their importance. The French court was often portrayed as a place of sexual freedoms, and Marie Antoinette became the target of insulting pamphlets and caricatures before her execution during the French Revolution. KK

Snowshill Manor, Gloucestershire · Pair of garters · *1775-1800 · Brass, silk · 30.5 x 1.8cm · Inscribed: 'Je peins une beauté fidèle; Je forme un emsemble parfait' (I paint a beauty that is faithful; I form a perfect whole) and 'Et quand je trace ce portrait, Vous seule en êtes le modèle' (And when I draw this portrait, you alone are the model) · NT 1350074*

The queen of crime

This sinister jar in the shape of a human skull belonged to the archaeologist Sir Max Mallowan (1904–78), the second husband of crime writer Agatha Christie (1890–1976). They shared many interests, including a love of ceramics, and a fine collection survives at their summer home, Greenway in Devon. Many of the pieces were bought, although some were taken from archaeological digs overseas.

The naturalistic jar was made in Japan in the late 19th century and Mallowan is believed to have stored his tobacco inside it. Perched on the lid is a ceramic frog, sometimes seen as a symbol of luck and prosperity. The contrast of the living frog with the skull is possibly a reference to the cycle of life and death in Japanese Buddhism. It is not known exactly when the jar came to Greenway, but it is listed in an inventory taken just before the property was requisitioned by the American Coastguard in 1942.

Is this a novelty that appealed to the 'Queen of Crime', or is it a reminder of mortality and the fragility of human life? Skulls were commonly used as memento mori (Latin for 'remember you must die'), a suitable subject for a crime writer. KK

Greenway, Devon · Skull jar with frog finial on lid ·
Late 19th century · Stoneware · 12 x 13 x 16.6cm · NT 118607

All the world's a stage

The playwright George Bernard Shaw (1856–1950) disliked fuss about his birthdays. He received many unwanted gifts from admirers, including a bison's foot inkstand and a personalised box of chocolates, which he donated to the local village fete. In 1936, his friends at the Malvern Festival (founded to stage Shaw's plays) discussed possible presents for his 80th birthday. Shaw thanked them but suggested only token gifts from Woolworths that cost no more than threepence. He preferred useful gifts rather than expensive trifles and admired new department stores, which provided low-cost goods for a mass market.

Shaw was delighted with his personal and amusing Woolworths presents, which included a coat hanger from actress Wendy Hiller (star of the 1938 film *Pygmalion*), sealing wax and a razorblade. This metal pencil sharpener in the shape of a globe was the gift of actress Mavis Walker, who gave it to him during rehearsals at the festival. Contemporary photographs show it in use on Shaw's desk in his famous revolving writing hut, where it can still be seen today. KK

Shaw's Corner, Hertfordshire · Pencil sharpener · *F.W. Woolworth & Co. Ltd* · *1936* · *Metal* · *4.7 x 4.1cm* · *NT 1274987*

Battle of the bards

George Bernard Shaw (1856–1950) was a prolific
writer from the 1880s until his death in 1950.
He had long been interested in the works of
Shakespeare and echoed Shakespearian themes
in his works, even controversially claiming his
work was 'better than Shakespeare'. When
puppeteer Waldo Lanchester (1897–1978) showed
Shaw two puppets he had made and invited him
to write a short drama for them, the result was a
ten-minute Punch-and-Judy-style sketch, *Shakes
versus Shav*. This comic argument between the
two playwrights – during which they physically
fight over which is greater – was first performed
in Malvern in August 1949.

   The puppets were carved in wood and Shaw
– or 'Shav' – was dressed in a brown Norfolk
jacket. Lanchester created four other puppets
for the play, representing characters created
by Shaw and Shakespeare, including Macbeth.
On the magic of marionettes, Shaw wrote that
while there was 'nothing wonderful in a living
actor moving and speaking … that wooden-
headed dolls should do so is a marvel that
never palls'. KK

Shaw's Corner, Hertfordshire · George Bernard Shaw
puppet · *Waldo S. Lanchester* · 1949 · *Textile and wood* ·
53cm (height) · NT 1275141

Lifeboat bravery

On a stormy evening in October 1891, the French ship *Henri et Leontine* crashed onto the rocks near Brook on the Isle of Wight. After several unsuccessful attempts to launch the lifeboat in rough seas, a 23-year-old crew member called Jack bravely swam out to the wreck with a line. Jack – actually John Seely, later first Baron Mottistone (1868–1947) – helped the badly injured captain ashore. He was later presented with the ship's wooden figurehead, as well as the French Medaille d'Honneur, for his daring rescue.

In the early 19th century, some 1,800 ships were wrecked each year around the British and Irish coasts. In 1824 the Royal National Institution for the Preservation of Life from Shipwreck (today called the RNLI) was formed, helping coastal communities to provide an organised rescue service and save lives at sea. Brook Lifeboat Station was established in 1860 and Jack Seely, who became a politician and distinguished soldier, was on the crew for over 40 years. He served as coxswain in the 1930s, while living at Mottistone Manor. KK

Mottistone Estate, Isle of Wight · Ship's figurehead · *Unknown French maker · 1873 · Wood · 96 x 35 x 33cm · NT 1412308 · Given to the National Trust in 1964*

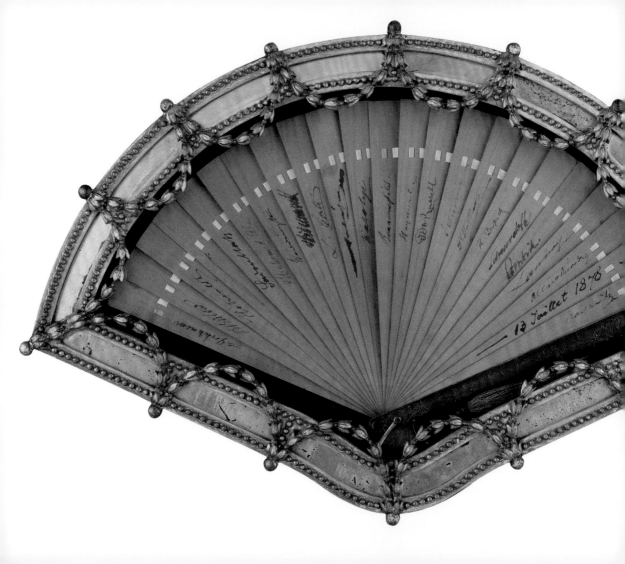

A symbol of peace

This cherrywood fan hanging on the wall at Hughenden is a statesman's souvenir. It was presented to Prime Minister Benjamin Disraeli (1804–81) at the conclusion of the Congress of Berlin in 1878. A power struggle was taking place in the eastern Mediterranean between Russia, other European powers and the declining Ottoman (Turkish) Empire. The leaders of Europe were invited to Berlin by German chancellor Otto von Bismarck (1815–98) to discuss these conflicts over territory. Despite ill health, Disraeli joined the negotiations and was actively involved in redrawing European borders.

The Ottoman delegate, Mahomet Ali, was delighted with the outcome of the congress.

He presented this fan to Disraeli as a keepsake in gratitude for his diplomacy, and each member of the congress signed a blade. For Disraeli, the fan – now displayed at his former home in Buckinghamshire – symbolised 'peace with honour' in Europe. Yet many resented the outcomes of the congress, and the decisions made in restructuring the borders of southern Europe would sow the seeds of future conflicts. KK

Hughenden, Buckinghamshire · Fan · *13 July 1878* ·
Cherrywood, gilt, glass, velvet · 35.5 x 55.9cm · NT 428696

'Winkle up'

The Winkle Club of Hastings was founded in 1900 by a group of local fishermen. To this day, every member (or 'Winkler') is obliged to carry a winkle shell with them, which they must produce when asked by a fellow member to 'winkle up'. Failure to do so results in a fine (£1 at the time of going to print), with all funds raised going to local causes.

In 1955, the year after he retired from his second term as prime minister, Sir Winston Churchill (1874–1965) was invited to become a member of the club. At a time when he was offered countless honours from organisations around the world, many requests had to be declined. When the invitation from the Winkle Club arrived, however, he accepted straight away, saying: 'This is one thing I want to do.'

Traditionally, members of the club carried either a hollow winkle or one filled with wax. Befitting his status as a 'Distinguished Member', however, Churchill's was made from solid gold. KC

Chartwell, Kent · Golden winkle · *1955* · *Gold (not hallmarked)* · *1.5 x 2 x 2cm* · *NT 1102834*

Panda-monium

In the winter of 1938–9, the arrival of a panda cub called Ming at London Zoo caused a sensation in the British press. Ming was celebrated as 'the Shirley Temple of the animal world', and Winston Churchill (1874–1965) was invited to meet her by Julian Huxley (1887–1975), Secretary of the Zoological Society. Churchill later remarked that the visit 'exceeded all my expectations … and they were very high!'

This toy panda was thought to date from that visit but recent research has revealed not only that Churchill owned it prior to Ming's arrival, but that it was in fact the outer case of a hot-water bottle. Churchill reportedly told Huxley that he owned a hot-water bottle cover made of faux panda fur. His youngest daughter also recalled that he had 'a much-loved panda hot-water bottle cover'. The original bottle has not survived but the panda continued to be used by Churchill's secretaries when a book was removed from a shelf, marking the spot to which it should be returned. KC

Chartwell, Kent · Churchill's toy panda · *Early 20th century · Faux fur, glass · 19 x 12 x 23cm · NT 1100838*

Rock star

Billed in 1859 as the 'biggest rock in the world', the Bowder Stone is a natural curiosity that has fascinated visitors to the Borrowdale valley since the 18th century.

The giant boulder, detached from the crags above, rests on a knife edge, seemingly about to topple at any moment. After it was bought by the wealthy Joseph Pocklington in 1798, a ladder was installed so that visitors could scale this little mountain, with its stunning views of the valley. Pocklington transformed the site into a Druidic attraction, adding a hermit's hut, a standing stone and a cottage. An elderly custodian was installed in the cottage, charging a small fee to scale the ladder. The stone became an essential part of 19th-century Lake District tourism, and writers and artists, including John Ruskin (1819–1900), left records of their encounters with it.

The custodian has gone, but a ladder remains, and when it's too wet to climb Scafell Pike, England's highest mountain, you can climb the biggest rock in the world instead. HW

Borrowdale, Cumbria · The Bowder Stone · *18.65m (length), 1,273 tonnes*

Pre-Raphaelite props

Pre-Raphaelite painter and poet Dante Gabriel Rossetti (1828–82) lived at 16 Cheyne Walk, Chelsea, from 1862 until his death. He filled the early Georgian house with antique furniture, Chinese and Japanese porcelain, Eastern carpets, metalwork and other beautiful objects. Rossetti was interested in unusual and striking pieces. This winged urn and basin were among the items from his eclectic collection that found their way into his pictures, as he used and reused them as props in his compositions.

The urn appears repeatedly in Rossetti's work in the 1860s and 1870s, in both studies and finished pictures. It may not have started life together with the basin, and Rossetti didn't always use them in that way. In *Washing Hands* (1865, opposite) they appear together, with a young woman washing her hands. In *La Bella Mano* (1875) the urn reappears, but with its wings relocated around the figure on top. A young woman is again washing her hands, but in a quite different basin. Modern visitors may see a resemblance to the Golden Snitch from the wizarding world of Harry Potter. SP

Wightwick Manor, Wolverhampton · Urn and basin · *Unknown maker and date* · *Brass and copper* · *Urn 36 x 36cm, basin 24 x 30 x 24cm · NT 1287168*

Right • *Washing Hands*, 1865, Dante Gabriel
Rossetti (1828–82), pencil and watercolour
on paper, 44.5 x 37.5cm, private collection.

6. TOOLS OF THE TRADE

Many properties in the care of the National Trust were places of work as well as homes. The Trust looks after the industrial mill at Quarry Bank (opposite), but also, on a more modest scale, a vast range of objects, pictures and documents linked to domestic and estate management roles. These include the message in a bottle left beneath the floorboards by an estate carpenter at Knole. The collections also contain examples of tools and techniques that show how work has changed over time.

Growth in commerce, global trading and technological advances all influenced changes in patterns of work. Human labour was increasingly replaced by machines that – like the donkey wheel – harnessed the power of animals, or used water and wind, and later steam and electricity. From the mid-1700s onwards, new machinery sped up production processes, as work moved away from the home and cottage industry into factory production. The development in 1767 of Richard Arkwright's water frame revolutionised textile production, shifting it away from small-scale production to mass manufacturing. Skilled hand-weavers used inventions such as the light-magnifying glass bowl to increase their hours of work at home. Technology saw the introduction of hundreds of factory workers operating machines and quality-testing mass-produced yarn and cloth. Quarry Bank was one of the first mills to be built when Arkwright's patent lapsed, and it made use of the latest innovations and machine technology. It is a remarkable survival of an industrial age.

This section also contains examples of industry and production spanning thousands of years, from ancient Egyptian tax receipts to a gardener's tools, an architect's model and a manual of sewing, complete with miniature garments.

Back taxes

At first glance these fragments look like unremarkable shards of broken pottery, but look closely and you will see that each one is covered in writing. Ancient Egyptian scribes used potsherds like scrap paper – for notetaking, calculations and receipts – because they were cheaper than papyrus. The potsherds are known as *ostraca*, a term originally derived from an ancient Greek word for the broken pottery used in votes to 'ostracise', or exile, unpopular community members.

These *ostraca* date from the 2nd and 3rd centuries AD, and most of the texts are written in Greek (the official language of Egypt at the time). They provide amazing insights into ancient lives. The texts include taxpayers' names and they describe the payment of taxes on income, taxes on utilities and fruit production, and a mortgage loan supplied by a local undertaker to two Roman citizens. There are over 200 *ostraca* at Kingston Lacy, which are believed to have been taken from the island of Elephantine, near Aswan in Egypt, during an expedition by collector William John Bankes (1786–1855). KK

Kingston Lacy, Dorset · Ostraca · *1–200AD* · Pottery · *Various dimensions* · *NT 1257846–1258055*

Donkey work

This enormous structure is a Tudor donkey wheel, a wonderful survival from the age of animal-powered machines. It is at Greys Court and sits over a medieval well, dug approximately 55 metres deep into the Oxfordshire chalk. As a donkey paced over the elm boards inside the vertical treadwheel, the water was slowly hoisted in large buckets from the well up to a tank on the roof. There, the bucket caught on a hook, which emptied the water into the tank for the household's use.

Animal and human-powered machines were common before the industrial age, when they were replaced with machines powered by water, wind, steam and electricity. This is the largest surviving donkey wheel in Britain and was built in 1586-7. It was still in use in the early 20th century. A smaller working example from the same period can be seen at Carisbrooke Castle on the Isle of Wight, where visitors can still enjoy short demonstrations by the castle donkeys. Another, later example is preserved at the National Trust's Saddlescombe Farm in Sussex. KK

Greys Court, Oxfordshire · Donkey wheel · *1586-7* · *Wood* · *c.600cm (diameter)* · *NT 198019*

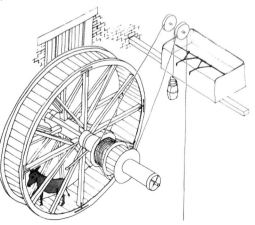

The corncrake's cry

When the jagged wheel is rolled across a surface, this gadget produces a rasping sound, like a comb scraped across a matchbox. The noise mimics the 'crex, crex' call of a corncrake, once a distinctive sound of summer, but today sadly rare. Corncrakes are about the same size as their relative the moorhen, and they were once widespread in the United Kingdom. The population of these migratory birds fell dramatically across Europe in the 20th century due to changes in land management, such as the cutting of grass crops earlier in the year. They are now a globally threatened species and their habitats are protected by conservation measures.

Corncrakes are secretive birds, more often heard than seen, but males are fiercely territorial. Callers made from wood or notched bone were used in the 19th and 20th centuries to mimic and lure birds. These were employed by both naturalists and hunters, who decoyed and shot corncrakes for food and the taxidermy trade. This wooden caller at Llanerchaeron is a poignant reminder of what has been lost, since no breeding pairs survive in Wales in the 21st century. KK

Llanerchaeron, Ceredigion · Bird caller · *Unknown maker and date · Wood (ash) · 14.3 x 4.1 x 4.5cm · NT 547848*

Assault on the senses

When this three-handled pot was excavated in 1986 at Corfe Castle and reassembled, its purpose was a mystery. Years later archaeologists shared a picture on social media and it was finally revealed to be a 17th-century firepot or 'stankpot' – an English Civil War stink bomb. Similar examples exist in the Netherlands and analysis of their contents reveals the presence of noxious substances, including sulphur, pitch and pepper seeds. A fuse was suspended from each handle; this was lit and the pot was lobbed through a window or over a wall like a hand grenade, where it would break and ignite. The fumes would cause panic and confusion – an assault on the senses – making the defenders more vulnerable to attack.

Grenades were widely used by both sides during the English Civil War and there are surviving examples of ceramic and metal hand grenades from this period. However, this is the only known stinkpot of its kind in Britain and it may be a Dutch import. Corfe Castle suffered a number of sieges before it surrendered and was 'slighted' (deliberately damaged to deny its use to the enemy) in 1646. KK

Corfe Castle, Dorset · Three-handled 'stankpot' · *1600–1700 · Ceramic · 15cm (height) · NT 420358*

A grave error

Everyone makes mistakes, as the stonemason carving this tombstone in 18th-century Shrewsbury could have attested. The hand-carved inscription, dated April 1731, was in memory of John Elsmere, son of Samuel Elsmere from Almond Park in Shrewsbury, and John's wife, Mary. Only part of the inscription survives, but it suggests the family's surname was a challenge, as it is twice misspelt, including once as 'Elsmare'.

Minor misspellings and spacing errors are not uncommon on gravestones, but because they were literally set in stone, they were hard to correct. This example survives because it was kept and recycled. It was discovered by National Trust staff on the underside of a heavy giltwood and marble-topped table at Powis Castle. This is one of three grand side tables, complete with large giltwood eagles, which were made in around 1740. Meanwhile, practice makes perfect and a correctly spelt memorial for the Elsmere family was recorded at the medieval church of St Mary's in Shrewsbury in 1825. KK

Powis Castle, Powys · One of three giltwood side tables · c.1740 · Giltwood, deal, marble · 92 x 128 x 47cm · NT 1181052.2 · ‡ 1963

Orchid mania

This perforated pot, found at Biddulph Grange Garden, may once have supported the aerial roots of rare orchids growing in a 'stove house'. During the 19th century, plant hunters wiped out entire orchid populations in the wild as they rushed to bring back prize specimens.

The former owner of Biddulph, James Bateman (1811–97), was an orchid enthusiast from an early age. While at university, he sponsored a plant-hunting expedition to South America, which brought over 60 orchid species back to Britain. Later, he published an enormous book devoted to orchids, featuring 40 life-sized hand-coloured illustrations, as well as a practical grower's guide.

Before Bateman moved to Biddulph in 1842, he lived at nearby Knypersley Hall in Staffordshire. A contemporary account describes the Knypersley orchid houses (opposite) and the elegant orchid pots, which had an 'abundance of holes' for plants to cling to and to allow air and moisture to circulate. This pot may have travelled with Bateman to his new home at Biddulph, where he created a globally inspired garden complete with a Victorian vision of China and Egypt. KK

Biddulph Grange Garden, Staffordshire · Plant support · *1830–70 · Terracotta or earthenware · 40cm (height)* · *NT 104645*

Are you sitting comfortably?

This chair was the perfect gift for a leisure-loving 18th-century gentleman. Fitted into the chair is an adjustable wooden slope or rest, angled to provide a writing surface or comfortably hold a book. Often known as a reading chair, the innovative design saw the user sit back-to-front on the seat, resting their arms on the padded top rail and facing the wooden slope. It is found in the grand library at Kedleston Hall, one of a suite of state rooms designed by architect Robert Adam (1728–92) for the Curzon family to impress their visitors. It is an example of the Georgians' love of 'metamorphic' or multi-purpose furniture.

The chair dates to about 1730, but similar designs were still being made almost a century later. The large size of the rest suggests this chair could also have been used for painting or drawing. Reading and art both played important roles in 18th-century society, to entertain guests as well as to demonstrate cultural knowledge. Under each arm is a small swing-out drawer with compartments, possibly for ink or paints, with another drawer concealed under the seat. KK

Kedleston Hall, Derbyshire · Reading or artist's chair ·
Unknown English maker · c.1730 · Mahogany, beech, oak, leather, horsehair, brass studs · 109 x 74 x 97cm · NT 108612 · Purchased with the aid of a grant from the National Heritage Memorial Fund · ‡ 1988

Miniature memorial

In 1905 near York Minster, a war memorial was unveiled to those who served and were lost in the South African War (or Second Boer War, 1899–1902). It contains the names of almost 1,500 Yorkshire soldiers, sailors and nurses, many of whom died from disease rather than in battle. This is a model of the original design by architect George Bodley (1827–1907) and features the figures of service personnel, including a nurse clutching bandages. The model is not identical to its life-sized equivalent, as Bodley redesigned the sailor figure to hold a length of chain or rope, rather than a gun.

The model was given to Frank Green, the secretary of the committee that raised funds for the memorial. Green bought and restored Treasurer's House in the centre of York and opened it in 1900 to raise money for the wounded. Although war memorials were tributes funded by fellow citizens, some families felt the money could have been better used. Unemployment was a challenge for returning volunteer soldiers and many had to sell furniture or even wedding rings to buy food. KK

Treasurer's House, York · War memorial model · *Studio of George Frederick Bodley* · *c.1905* · *Wood* · *40.6 x 21.6cm* · *NT 592874*

Shine a light

This simple glass bowl boasts no intricate details or hidden decoration, but when filled with water and placed in front of a burning candle it could reflect light around a room. Although a poor substitute for natural light, a weaver's bowl traditionally allowed 19th-century agricultural workers and farmers to work into the evening, at a time when the textile industry relied on hand-weaving at home. Hand-weaving supplemented the income of farmers and farm workers. With the ability to make one candle last longer into a dark evening, the weaver's bowl would have been a critical aid for a working family.

The middle-class Browne family of Townend, who owned this example, would not have relied on it for income, although their tenants might have had similar devices. When the family or their servants did use the bowl for extra light, it may have been for embroidery, or mending clothes. Although perhaps curious to modern eyes, the weaver's bowl literally shines a light on the struggles of rural workers, and their need to stretch every resource – even candlelight – to its utmost. HA

Townend, Cumbria · Hand-blown glass bowl with a circular base and lip · *1800–1900* · *Glass* · *25.4 (height) x 20cm (diameter)* · *NT 478148*

A stitch in time

Tucked inside the pages of this book are tiny garments, including miniature socks, shirts and a knitted nightcap. These were 'specimens', examples of needlework projects to demonstrate sewing skills and understanding of techniques. Needlework was considered to be an important part of girls' education for hundreds of years, and this workbook was particularly designed to help poorer pupils in Ireland's schools to gain practical skills. The instruction book, with its 'simple directions for plain and fancy works', was produced by the National Model Female School in Dublin using samples made by pupils.

The chapters are set out by degree of difficulty, beginning with basic sewing and hemming before progressing to more advanced techniques such as buttonholes, knitting and embroidery. Each specimen page includes a reference showing where to find the step-by-step explanation of the featured stitch. It is one of thousands of items generously donated to the Springhill Costume Collection. Many of them were made by hand and demonstrate the techniques and skills taught in this workbook. KK

Springhill, County Londonderry · Book of specimens · *National Model Female School and unknown pupils* · *1846* · *Paper, textile · 23 x 18.5 x 7cm · NT 604937*

Testing times

Lancashire dominated the global production and trade of cotton textiles during the 19th and early 20th centuries, with the industrial city of Manchester nicknamed 'Cottonopolis'. Imported cotton harvested by enslaved people was twisted or spun into a strong yarn, which was woven into cloth. Mills such as Quarry Bank – founded by entrepreneur Samuel Greg (1758–1834) in 1784 – used newly invented water- and steam-powered machines to spin yarn and produce cloth in huge quantities.

With new industry came new challenges, because some merchants supplied poor-quality or 'short-reeled' yarn. Testing houses were established to regulate the yarn and cloth to required standards, with new scientific instruments developed to measure the strength, weight and twist-count of textiles. By the 1890s, Quarry Bank had its own testing room to quality-check incoming and outgoing yarn and cloth. This wrap wheel would have been a standard piece of equipment. When the handle was turned, a pre-determined length of yarn was wound evenly around the frame, and could then be assessed and weighed. A mechanical counter showed the number of rotations. This wheel was made locally by Dronsfield Brothers in Oldham, and the design was patented in August 1916. KK

Quarry Bank, Cheshire · Wrap wheel · *Dronsfield Brothers Ltd · 1915 · Wood, metal · 54 x 73 x 41cm · NT 1454070*

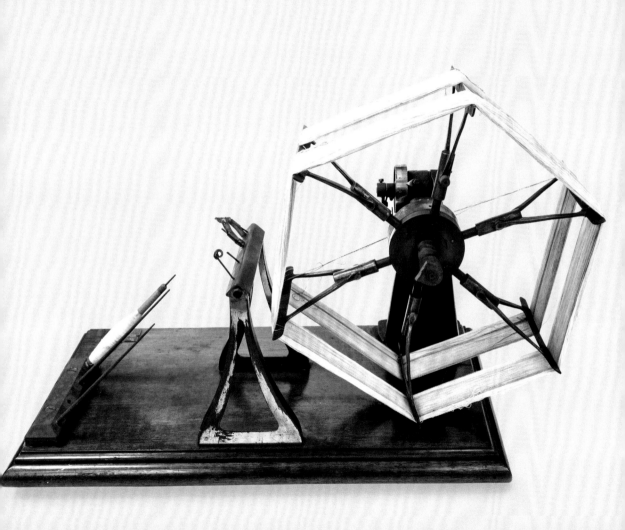

The price of progress

Quarry Bank near Manchester is one of the best-preserved textile mills of the Industrial Revolution. Founded by the Greg family in 1784, by the 1860s it was the headquarters of one of the largest cotton-manufacturing businesses in the world. Records show there were more than 400 millworkers at Quarry Bank, and simple wooden or tin cups like these would have been used on a Friday to collect their weekly wages.

A working day at Quarry Bank could last 14½ hours, with perhaps 90 minutes of breaks. While many roles in the cotton industry had fixed hourly wages, weavers were paid different amounts each week – known as 'piece rate' – according to the amount and quality of cloth they had produced. Pay also depended on experience and the number of machines a person could run. A proportion of wages was deducted for cottage rents and purchases in the mill-owned shop. Poor working conditions – with noisy machinery and air filled with cotton dust – could also be detrimental to workers' health, so a percentage of wages went into a 'sick club', formed in 1817. KK

Quarry Bank, Cheshire · Tray and 50 wage cups ·
1800–1900 · Wood · Various dimensions · NT 1460621

Message in a bottle

In 2017, archaeology volunteers at Knole in Kent spotted the shape of a bottle in the dust beneath the floorboards. Carefully brought to the surface with the aid of a vacuum cleaner, it was found to be a Perrier bottle containing a rolled-up piece of embossed Knole paper. A handwritten note on the paper read: 'Sept 26th 1906. This bottle was dropted here in the year AD 1906 by S.G. Doggett when these Radiators were put in, also the Hot Water Service.'

The name matched some graffiti found in a nearby room and, through the Knole Oral History database, the team identified the author as Sidney George Doggett (1884–1967). Doggett was born at Knole and was the estate carpenter there for 62 years. When news of the discovery was made public, members of his family visited Knole to share memories and later generously donated his original toolbox to the Trust, complete with over 100 tools (NT 131699). This small floorboard find gives a wonderful insight into the layers of history at Knole, and the stories of those who have lived and worked there. KK

Knole, Kent · Message in a Perrier bottle · *S.G. Doggett · 1906 · Glass, paper, newspaper · 22cm (height) · NT 131998*

7. FEELING PLAYFUL

Throughout history, when essential work is finished, people have found time for play. Toys have developed alongside technological advances but some have changed remarkably little over the centuries. From hobby horses and skittles to politically motivated pop-up toys, this section explores playful and imaginative creations.

Some of the curiosities here were invented by imaginative minds, including Beatrix Potter and Rudyard Kipling. Humour and illusion also play a role in many decorative schemes across National Trust properties and collections. Playful objects such as 'anamorphic' (two-way) paintings, the

tinder lighter that resembles a pistol, the toy suffragette (opposite) or the 'tortoise-shell' cat carved in the stonework at Knightshayes, reveal a sense of humour. The strange statuary at Lacock Abbey in Wiltshire features everything from a grinning skeleton to a sugar cube balanced in jest on the terracotta nose of a goat.

As well as developing social skills and occupying time, play was also seen as an important tool for education and health. The miniature library is an early example of encouraging learning through play, while Tudor tennis balls found in a long gallery reveal the early history of a familiar sport.

The Doctor's deadly enemy

It isn't every day you see one of the famous Time Lord's greatest enemies while visiting a National Trust property. This iconic monster – a menacing Dalek, renowned for its sinister cry, 'Exterminate!' – entered the collection in 2018 as an example of the impact of television on childhood experiences. Daleks first appeared on screen in 1963 and became an instant hit, sparking a craze known as 'Dalekmania'. Over the years, these extraterrestrial creatures made regular appearances in the BBC science-fiction television series *Doctor Who*, becoming a familiar feature of many childhoods.

The Dalek was operated from the inside using a series of handles and levers. This bronze drone Dalek ('No. 4') featured in the revived BBC series in 2005, appearing on screen in the episodes 'Bad Wolf' and 'The Parting of the Ways'. During these episodes the ninth Doctor (played by Christopher Eccleston) and his companions unmask a plot to 'harvest' humans to make new Daleks. The plan is scuppered but the Doctor, who only narrowly escapes destruction, regenerates into his tenth incarnation (played by David Tennant). KK

The Children's Country House at Sudbury, Derbyshire
• Dalek • *2004/5* • *Fibreglass resin composite, wood, paint, rubber and plastic* • *165 x 90 x 140cm* • *NT 671987*

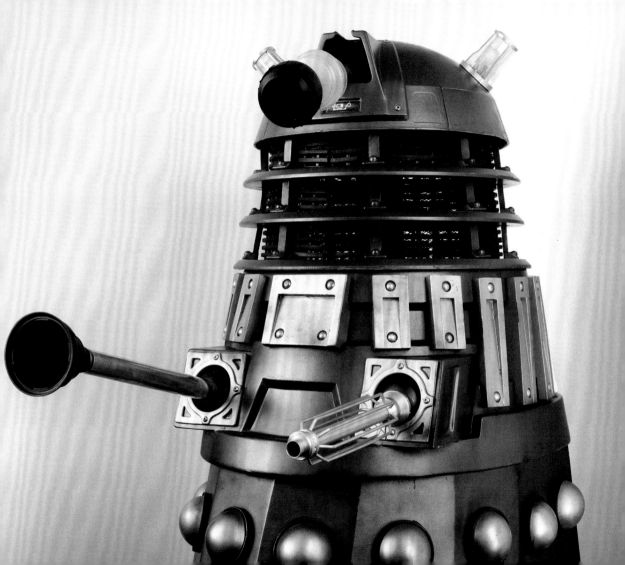

'The cleverest bit of work'

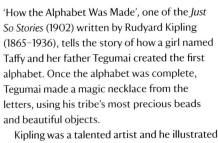

'How the Alphabet Was Made', one of the *Just So Stories* (1902) written by Rudyard Kipling (1865–1936), tells the story of how a girl named Taffy and her father Tegumai created the first alphabet. Once the alphabet was complete, Tegumai made a magic necklace from the letters, using his tribe's most precious beads and beautiful objects.

Kipling was a talented artist and he illustrated the necklace in the story himself. Sir Percy Bates (1879–1946), then editor of *The Morning Post*, commissioned a jeweller to create a necklace based on Kipling's drawing. Bates pretended he had taken the 'original necklace' from Kipling's house, Bateman's, for repair. Kipling played along, describing the necklace as 'one of the most beautiful pieces of Neolithic art that has ever been produced'.

Bates brought the necklace to Bateman's, framed in a special presentation case, in 1928. After receiving the gift, Kipling described it as 'absolutely the prettiest and cleverest bit of work I've ever seen, and I nearly had a fit when I looked at the photo and my original drawing'. HM

Bateman's, East Sussex · Necklace · *Captain Spink, jeweller · 1927 · Wood, stone, metal and organic materials · 80cm (length) with charms of various dimensions ·* NT 760463

Bowled over

This playful set of Edwardian skittles is modelled on performing circus animals. Eight of the bear skittles, with thick brown fur, represent the common grizzly. The ninth skittle represents its closest relative, the polar bear, and is dressed in a red felt jacket and – appropriately for the 'kingpin' – a crown. These skittles were used to play the medieval game of ninepin, with eight skittles placed in a diamond shape and the red skittle positioned in the centre. Attempts to bowl them over sent the bears joyfully dancing and spinning around the floor. The rings through the bears' noses may allude to the performing bears once popular in American circus acts.

This game was among childhood possessions belonging to the 10th Earl of Stamford, Roger Grey (1896–1976), and his sister, Lady Jane (1899–1991), who moved to Dunham Massey in 1910. The skittle design is very similar to that of the famous stuffed toys created by Margarete Steiff (1847–1909), who launched the popular Steiff toy brand with a felt elephant in 1880, followed by a menagerie of monkeys, donkeys, mice, dogs, cats, rabbits, giraffes and other cuddly creations. EC

Dunham Massey, Cheshire · Set of nine individual toy bear skittles · *Unknown maker, possibly Steiff · c.1900 · Wood, textile, glass, metal · 21.5cm (height) · NT 937035*

Jailbreak

From this brick-like wooden box, a woman springs from her jail boldly waving a flag that reads 'Votes for Women'. Sold between 1909 and 1914 by Holborn department store Gamages, it belonged to a series of mechanical toys showing the struggle between the militant suffragettes – who used tactics such as window-smashing to demand the vote on equal terms with men – and the police.

These toys were not pro- or anti-suffrage, but were a way of poking fun at the political goings-on of the day. Still, it is the suffragette whose portrayal is cruel and unflattering, while the brutality of her imprisonment is ignored. The toy may have been a gift for Roger and Jane Grey, children of the 9th Earl and Countess of Stamford.

Gamages may have mocked the suffragettes by selling this toy, but they soon found themselves targeted. On the night of 28 January 1913, as part of a window-smashing campaign, suffragette Margaret James broke three of the department store's windows, racking up a repair bill of £60 (the equivalent of around £5,000 today). HA

Dunham Massey, Cheshire · Suffragette wooden toy · *Sold by Gamages · c.1909–14 · Ceramic, cardboard, metal · 29cm (height) · NT 937229*

Anyone for tennis?

Long narrow halls or galleries were fashionable in Tudor and Jacobean manor houses. They were used for indoor exercise, social gatherings and even games. At Little Moreton Hall, the Long Gallery is perched precariously at the top of the house, and centuries of repair and conservation have revealed clues about how it was used. Since the 1970s, four tennis balls have been discovered under floorboards and behind the Tudor panelling in the gallery. The first find, made of leather and filled with plant material, possibly moss or bracken, was dated by experts to the 17th century.

Tudor tennis was an indoor game, with balls played off walls and floors, so the Long Gallery may have been an ideal space. The earliest tennis balls were usually made of soft materials because they were struck by hand, but by the late 16th century tennis rackets were common. Tudor players often preferred specially made French tennis balls, which were crafted with wool wadding and leather. While few written accounts of life at Little Moreton Hall exist, these wonderful survivals give us a glimpse into the history of the house and its inhabitants. KK

Little Moreton Hall, Cheshire · Tennis ball · *17th century* · *Leather, plant material* · *5.5cm (diameter)* · *NT 282428.4*

Two for the price of one

Look straight ahead at this portrait of a young woman and an interloper appears. The head of a green parrot emerges just above her ear, where a hair accessory might sit. Move to the left and right and all becomes clear. This is a two-way or 'anamorphic' painting, in which two separate pictures – here a lady and a parrot – come into focus when it is viewed from different angles. The parrot may be the sitter's pet, or a symbolic image.

To achieve this optical effect, the artist painted on two facets of a series of prism-shaped vertical strips of wood, with the remaining facet applied to the backing. Early examples of these painterly curiosities date to the late 16th century, and references to 'turning pictures' are even to be found in Shakespeare. This painting hangs in a passageway at Clevedon Court, no doubt eliciting frequent double takes from passers-by. ARW

Clevedon Court, North Somerset · Two-way painting, with woman and parrot · *British (English) School · c.1720–40 · Oil paint on wood laid on panel · 50.8 x 36.2cm · NT 624189 · ‡ 1998*

A curious cat

Beneath the staircase gallery at Knightshayes a strange creature with a cat's head and a tortoise's body seems to emerge from the wall. This carved stone corbel is a visual pun, a rebus: it represents a 'tortoise-shell cat'. Its designer, William Burges (1827–81), had a vivid creative imagination inspired by his passion for the art and architecture of the Middle Ages. Burges would have been familiar with the widespread medieval use of the rebus, a visual play on words often used to represent family names and in heraldry.

Burges's designs are full of animals, birds and plants. Other gallery corbels include a monkey clutching its long tail and a chick emerging from its shell menaced by a rat. Sculpture, mostly executed by Thomas Nicholls (c.1825–96) and his specialist carvers, was an important part of Burges's buildings. Knightshayes – the only complete country house Burges designed – was built for Sir John Heathcoat Amory, 1st Baronet (1829–1914), between 1869 and 1874. The sculpture was largely completed but the rest of Burges's extravagant interior designs were rejected. SP

Knightshayes, Devon · Corbel of a tortoise-shell cat · *William Burges · 1869–74 · Probably modelled by Thomas Nicholls and carved by one of his craftsmen · Carved stone · 17 x 11cm (whole corbel 30 x 19 x 23cm) · NT 541998*

With sugar on top

Arguably the strangest statuary in England can be found in the Gothick entrance hall of Lacock Abbey. The 27 sculptures populating its walls include a bust of a bull, crowned and sporting a ruffled shirt; a wizard in a pointed hat; the Greek philosopher Diogenes searching for the truth; and the torso of the angel of death, as a grinning winged skeleton (see page 13). Ela, Countess of Salisbury (1187–1261, the Abbey's founder), Old Testament prophets, and figures from local medieval history complete the scheme.

The sculptures were made in 1755–6 by the mysteriously untraceable Victor Alexander Sederbach (active 1755–7), whose style suggests south German or Austrian origin. John Ivory Talbot (?1691–1772), Lacock's then owner, recounted that Sederbach modelled the figures directly in terracotta and baked them in the Abbey orchard to make them 'ring like a Garden-pot'. No other statuary by Sederbach has ever been identified.

The goat accompanying the figure of Aaron balances a real sugar cube on its nose. The first sugar cube was reputedly placed there as a joke by a visiting student over 100 years ago. ARW

Lacock Abbey, Wiltshire · Set of 27 figures and busts · *Victor Alexander Sederbach · 1755–6 · Terracotta · Various dimensions · NT 996395–996421*

Faux firepower

This may look like an oddly shaped pistol, but it is actually a cleverly concealed lighter. Before the invention of reliable matches in Europe in the 19th century, households relied on flint, steel and tinder (dry material such as wood shavings or grass) to create a flame and keep fires burning in the hearth. Lighting a fire could be time-consuming and by the 18th century flintlock tinder lighters, or 'strike-a-lights', were popular in wealthy households. This one at Felbrigg Hall was made by the Nocks, a famous family of London gunsmiths, and is inscribed 'A W Jan. 6th 1816' – although the owner of the initials remains a mystery.

Tinder lighters were innovative, practical and portable. When the trigger is pulled, the flintlock mechanism strikes the flint against the steel 'frizzen' to generate sparks. Unlike a flintlock pistol, where the sparks fall into a pan of gunpowder, igniting the main charge of powder inside the barrel to fire a projectile, in the case of the lighter the sparks fall into a pan of dry tinder. This flame lights a candle, fitted in the attached candleholder.

Electricity was not installed at Felbrigg Hall until 1954 because the owner, Robert Wyndham Ketton-Cremer (1906–69), liked the restful light of oil lamps and candles. KK

Felbrigg Hall, Norfolk · Lighter · *Henry Nock (active 1770–1804) or Samuel Nock (active 1800–51)* · *Iron, brass, wood* · *13 x 17.2 x 8.5cm* · *Inscribed: 1816* · *NT 1400345*

Playing the long game

There are several hobby horses and rocking horses in the National Trust's collections, but at almost 2.5 metres long this one is unique. Wooden stick horses have been used as children's toys for centuries. They are usually made of a pole or plank with a fabric or painted horse's head attached to one end. Some versions had a seat or, like this one, wheels. The 'rider' sat astride the stick and raised the horse's head using handles or reins.

This curious contraption may be a homemade joke, with a carved rocking horse's head and wheels playfully added to an extra-long wooden 'body'. A 20th-century inventory describes it as a Victorian hobby horse for several children. It is not known whether the horse was at Chastleton House in the 19th century, when it was home to the Whitmore family and their seven children. It now stands proudly in the 22-metre Long Gallery, which was once used for indoor exercise. Visitors are invited to guess how many children could ride it at any one time. KK

Chastleton House, Oxfordshire · Hobby horse · *Possibly 19th century · Wood, horsehair, paint · 248 x 21cm · NT 1430313*

Tiny titles

This adorable set of miniature books in its own wooden 'bookcase' box is one of the earliest examples of a miniature library for children. It was produced by London publisher John Marshall (active 1783–1828) in the early 1800s. Early children's books often had a religious purpose or were used to teach spelling, but these miniature libraries were marketed to entertain as well as educate. Marshall, who styled himself 'The Children's Printer', also made cabinets of picture-cards and puzzles, responding to fashionable ideas about learning through play.

There are 20 tiny textbooks by Marshall at A la Ronde – some the size of a matchbox – on subjects including geography, arithmetic and the histories of birds and insects. Marshall was inspired by the work of other children's publishers such as Thomas Boreman (active 1730–43), who produced ten miniature works playfully named his 'Gigantick' books. This little library at A la Ronde contains some of Boreman's books too, including a tiny illustrated text on the 'curious' animals found in the first zoo in London. These latter texts were owned by Polly Walrond (1747–72), who wrote her name inside some of the covers when aged about five or six. KK

A la Ronde, Devon · Set of miniature books in a library box · *John Marshall and Thomas Boreman* · *c.1800* · *Paper, wood* · *Various dimensions; box 31.5 x 18 x 10cm* · *NT 1312597.1–.32*

Miniature marvels

The Tale of Two Bad Mice by Beatrix Potter (1866–1943) tells the story of two naughty mice, Hunca Munca and Tom Thumb, who wreak havoc in a dolls' house. Potter's own pet mice – including one of her favourites, called Hunca Munca – provided the inspiration for the story.

Over the course of writing *Two Bad Mice*, the letters between Beatrix Potter and her publisher, Norman Warne (1868–1905), reveal a burgeoning friendship. Warne was an accomplished amateur carpenter. He built his niece an impressive dolls' house and sent photographs to Potter so that she could copy it for her illustrations (right). He also made a box with a glass front for her mice, so that she could observe them playing.

Potter received a parcel of dolls' house toys from Hamley's, sent by Warne, in February 1904. She wrote in thanks: '… the things will all do beautifully; the ham's appearance is enough to cause indigestion. I am getting almost more treasures than I can squeeze into one small book.' Tom Thumb, however, was less thrilled with the delicious-looking ham, soon discovering it was made of plaster. HA

Hill Top and Beatrix Potter Gallery, Cumbria · Dolls' house and contents · *Unknown maker, sold by Hamley's* · *c.1904* · *Wood, plaster, metal, paint* · *Various dimensions* · *Dolls' house NT 641707, plaster food NT 641577*

8. UNDERSTANDING THE WORLD

The collections in the National Trust's care are a wonderful resource for tracing humanity's changing understanding of the known world. These objects help us to explore knowledge and beliefs, from new scientific discoveries and travel to folklore and magic.

Protective charms such as witch bottles, witch balls and amulets have long been used to protect people, livestock and homes from spells or the 'evil eye' of passing witches. Alongside popular beliefs, new discoveries and new means to communicate through printing led to growing scientific understanding. Globes and maps were produced to help travellers physically and theoretically navigate a changing world, while scientific instruments enabled the measurement of everything from distance and temperature to rainfall or the number of hours of sunshine. Thanks to the research and experiments of individuals such as famous philosopher and mathematician Sir Isaac Newton, scientist Mary Ward and inventor William Armstrong, such discoveries changed the way we look at the world today.

Some of this new knowledge and technology had applications that were both practical and curious, such as electric jewels – an early example of wearable technology. The electrostatic Wimshurst influence machine was used by William Armstrong to create ghostly images of electrical discharges, while cheap printing enabled the spread of both factual news and sensational popular literature to an increasingly literate public.

Scientific scribbles

Are these childish etchings on the wall of Woolsthorpe Manor – some of them barely perceptible to the naked eye – the work of the young Sir Isaac Newton (1642–1727)? This modest farmhouse was his childhood home and it was here that the famous philosopher and mathematician made some of his most significant discoveries. He told several of his close friends that he conceived the law of gravity after watching an apple fall from a tree in the orchard.

Newton was fascinated by how things worked and was reportedly scolded for using charcoal on the white lime-washed walls at school to sketch out his ideas. When a post mill (an early type of windmill – similar to the model, shown right) was constructed nearby, he watched closely and even made a small working model operated by a mouse miller. Various geometrical drawings and scratch marks have been discovered at Woolsthorpe, including sketches of post mills like this one. In 2017 scientists using Reflectance Transformation Imaging discovered another drawing of a post

mill by the fireplace. Fittingly, this technology owes a great deal to Newton's own research, using light to capture surface information that is invisible to the naked eye. KK

Woolsthorpe Manor, Lincolnshire · Graffiti ·
Possibly Sir Isaac Newton · 17th century · Etched plaster ·
28 x 17.6cm · NT 427631

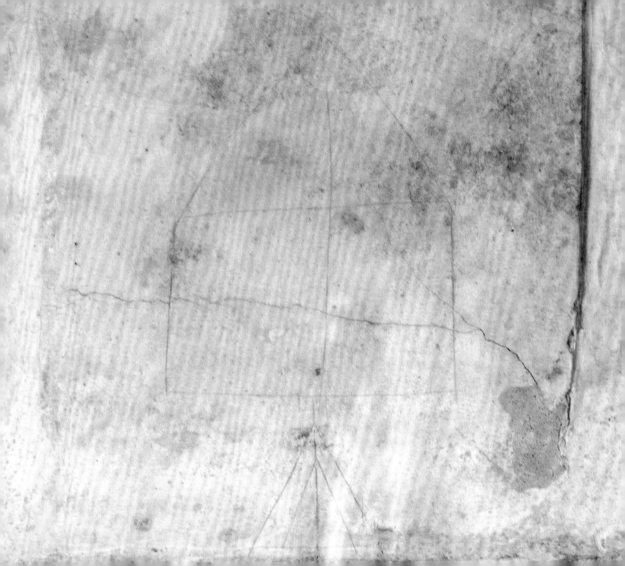

Under the lens

A microscope slide holding a scrap of hair, hand-labelled 'Wool of a Sardinian Dog', may seem an unusual object to find at a grand estate like Castle Ward. It is one of many that belonged to Mary Ward (1827–69) and her husband Henry, who made frequent visits to the family home where Mary pursued her scientific endeavours.

Encouraged by an early love of astronomy, Ward was given her first microscope aged 18. She explored the world both on a vast scale in the sky and, minutely, under a lens. Ward became a leading voice on these sciences, publishing books and popularising the subjects as hobbies for middle-class Victorians. She was allowed to receive the notices of the Royal Astronomical Society, and was even given special permission to enter the Royal Observatory at a time when it was against the rules for women to do so.

Sadly, this pioneering scientist is often best remembered for her tragic death – the first recorded motor-vehicle fatality. Her microscope, slides and watercolours at Castle Ward, however, tell of a woman who followed her passion and became an acknowledged expert in her field. HA

Castle Ward, County Down · Microscope slides · *Mary Ward · c.1860s · Glass and organic material · Each slide approx. 3 x 8cm · NT 835098 · Purchased in 1967 with a grant from the Ulster Land Fund*

Works like a charm

When this bottle was discovered beneath an old parish boundary wall on the Purbeck estate in Dorset, its contents were – unusually – still sealed inside. Analysis showed it contained a nauseating mix of nicotine, animal fat and salt water. This smelly concoction is believed to be a 'spell' or potion, which may have been intended to protect livestock from disease or malicious spirits in the 17th or 18th century.

Concealing items such as shoes, mummified cats or urine-filled bottles in hearths and walls might sound strange, but it was common practice in the 17th century, when it was widely believed to ward off evil spirits. Witches were often blamed for misfortune or ill health and witch bottles were intended to cause them pain and force them to reverse or remove their spells. Contemporary recipes recommended a combination of urine and sharp objects such as pins or nails, to be heated over a fire or buried. The effort required to create and conceal witch bottles is a testament to the extent of the popular belief in their power, and this example is a tangible link to the magical beliefs of the past. KK

Corfe Castle, Dorset · Witch bottle · *17th or 18th century* · *Glass, salt water, nicotine, animal fat · Approx. 15cm (height)* · *NT 420359*

If thine eye be evil

Amulets are objects believed to protect people from harm. This example, made in southern Italy or Spain, takes the form of a clenched right hand, the forefinger wrapped over the thumb to make the *mano fica* gesture. The gleaming crystal hand has a silver ring on the forefinger and is mounted onto a frilly gold cuff embellished with intricate enamelwork.

Mano fica translates literally as 'hand fig', *fica* being Italian slang for the female genitalia, and the gesture itself is an allusion to hetero-sexual intercourse. While the sign is considered offensive, its principal function as an amulet is to ward off the 'evil eye', a curse transmitted through a malicious and often envious glare that was widely believed to be capable of causing impotence or infertility. The *mano fica* has ancient origins and occurs in several cultures, but it is especially popular in southern Europe. In Spain such charms are known as *higa*. This precious example was made between about 1550 and 1650 and was probably given to a child to wear. ARW

Anglesey Abbey, Cambridgeshire · Amulet in the form of a clenched right hand · *Spanish or southern Italian* · *c.1550–1650* · *Crystal, gold, enamel* · *6.9 x 3.2cm* · *NT 517314*

Light reading

Chapbooks were small booklets of sensational stories or songs, particularly popular from the 17th to the 19th centuries. In common with modern comics and soap operas, illustrated chapbooks featured fables, historical tales and even saucy stories to amuse their readers. This popular reading material was sold by publishers and travelling pedlars called chapmen. Chapbooks were usually printed on one sheet of thin paper, so they were cheap to make and buy. Although they were printed in large numbers, very few survive today.

The chapbook shown here is one of several surviving at Townend that were collected over four centuries by a family of yeoman farmers. Their library reveals what they were reading from the 17th century onwards. The story in this case is inspired by a popular Tudor legend about a wealthy wounded knight who disguised himself as a beggar. Many versions were printed, but this unique 19th-century copy was produced locally in Ulverston. It is one of at least 45 books at Townend that are currently unrecorded anywhere else in the world. KK

Townend, Cumbria · The history of the blind beggar of Bethnal Green · *George Ashburner (printer)* · *c.1810* · *Paper and ink* · *15.8 x 10.3 x 0.2cm* · *NT 3172450*

The world in your pocket

Globes were state-of-the-art navigational aids in the 16th century. Up-to-date information was vital for travel and trade, helping people to plan the fastest and safest routes. While terrestrial globes represented the earth, celestial globes showed the heavens. This was especially important for sailors, who used the position of stars for navigation.

Pocket-sized globes were introduced to England in the 17th century and sold as status symbols and as educational tools for children. These hand-held navigational aids were often enclosed in a shagreen (fish-skin) case lined with a colourful map of the stars. This one at Buckland Abbey, former home of privateer Sir Francis Drake (1540–96), is marked with significant events in maritime history. These include the circumnavigation of the globe by naval officer George Anson (1697–1762), following in the footsteps of Drake's 16th-century world voyage. The site of the death of Captain James Cook (1728–79) in Hawaii is also marked. Cook was the first recorded European to visit many parts of the Pacific, mapping and

claiming land for the Crown. Globes such as this one drew on the depictions of coastline and islands that were recorded on his voyages. KK

Buckland Abbey, Devon · A New Globe of the Earth · *N. Lane · Late 18th century · Shagreen, wood, textile and paper · 7cm (diameter) · NT 809593*

Catching the rays

This Grade II listed glass globe once recorded hours of sunshine in the gardens at Cragside. The metal-mounted glass sphere concentrates sunlight onto a strong card marked with the hours of the day. As the sun travels across the sky, the rays are concentrated on the card and leave scorch marks, a visible record of the amount and intensity of sunlight. The results help scientists to understand and monitor changes in climate and weather. This sunshine recorder – sometimes known as a heliograph – was made locally in Newcastle by instrument makers Brady & Martin.

Cragside was home to inventor and engineer William, 1st Lord Armstrong (1810–1900). He was concerned about reliance on fossil fuels and interested in harnessing the power of the natural world, from hydroelectricity to the potential to use the sun's rays to generate energy. In 1876 his Newcastle workshop manufactured parts for a similar heliograph that was installed at the Royal Observatory in Greenwich. Although sunshine recorders were developed in the 19th century, some are still used by meteorologists today. A replica sphere now stands in the garden at Cragside. KK

Cragside, Northumberland · Sunshine recorder · *Brady & Martin of Newcastle · c.1880–1900 · Brass, glass · 28 x 21.5cm · NT 1232014 · ‡ 1977*

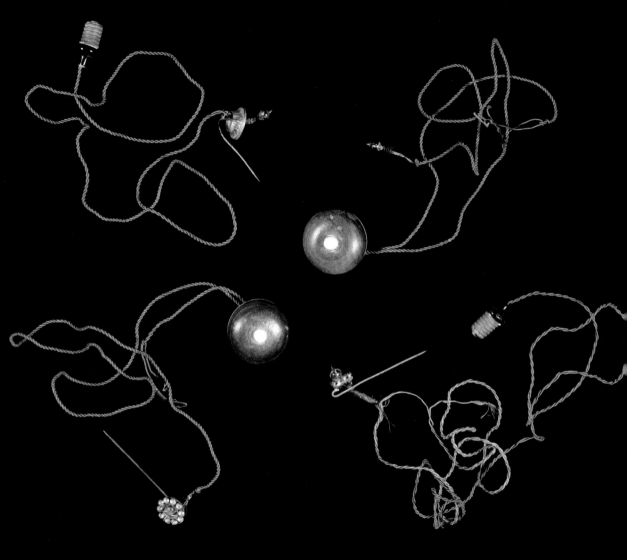

Wearable technology

This jewellery would literally have dazzled those who saw it. Inside each coloured glass jewel is a miniature four-volt bulb, powered by a battery hidden in the wearer's pocket or hair. When lit, the tiny lamps create the appearance of sparkling diamonds and rubies. Electric jewellery was developed by electrical genius Gustave Trouvé (1839–1902) in the 1870s and was used in spectacular theatre productions.

Today, wearable technology is common but in the 19th century 'decorative electricity' was a novelty. It was not without its dangers, because the heavy batteries could leak or overheat. Nonetheless, various hair adornments, scarf pins, tiaras and walking-stick jewels were developed. Power from the small battery usually lasted about 30 minutes and it was claimed that the larger jewels even gave enough light to read by. The electric jewels at Cragside were made in London and are thought to have belonged to the family of engineer and inventor William, 1st Lord Armstrong (1810–1900). The collection also includes a walking stick with a battery-powered light on its handle (NT 1232293). KK

Cragside, Northumberland · Electric jewellery · *Harvey & Peak · c.1880–1900 · Glass, metal · Displayed on cushion, 17 x 19cm · NT 1231065 · ‡ 1977*

The birth of the car

With leather upholstery and a 3.5 horsepower engine, this 1900 Benz was the cutting-edge technology of its time. Steam engines had been used since the 1700s to power road vehicles, but in 1886 a German engineer, Karl Benz (1844–1929), patented the world's first automobile. It used an internal-combustion engine, which burned fuel (petrol or gas) inside the engine, rather than in an external furnace. Benz sold licences for this new technology to other manufacturers, changing transport for ever.

This car was bought by motoring enthusiast Maurice Egerton, 4th Baron Egerton of Tatton (1874–1958), in the early 1900s. Egerton (right) bought the 'M1' vehicle registration in 1903, the first registration number in Cheshire, for a Darracq racing car. It was transferred to this 1900 Benz 'Comfortable' Vis-à-Vis following restoration work by his mechanic in the 1920s. Originally the petrol sat in an open pan under the driver's seat, until a carburettor was added. The right to use its M1 registration on public roads was sold in 2005 to generate funds for continued conservation and education at Tatton Park. The collection also contains an early electric car made in 1906. KK

Tatton Park, Cheshire · Car · *Benz 'Comfortable' Vis-à-Vis* · *1900* · *Brass, leather* · *233.7 x 210.8 x 137.1cm* · *NT 1298849*

Lightning machine

Have you ever touched something and seen a small spark? This electrostatic device – known as a Wimshurst machine – was invented in the 1880s to produce high-voltage static electricity. It works by rotating two glass discs (covered with small metal 'sectors') in opposite directions. This causes an imbalance of charges and creates a spark. Accumulated energy can be stored in Leyden jars. These machines became popular in late 19th- and early 20th-century laboratories for electrical experiments, and were also used in early X-ray research.

This machine and two Leyden jars can be found in the restored Electrical Room at Cragside, which was used by inventor William, 1st Lord Armstrong (1810–1900) as an experimental laboratory. His book *Electric Movement in Air and Water* (1897) contained photographs of the stunning patterns (usually invisible) produced by electrical discharges, which he generated with a Wimshurst machine. Armstrong's pioneering experiments, and the extraordinary images of them recorded by local photographer John Worsnop, have been reimagined for modern visitors to Cragside. KK

Cragside, Northumberland · Wimshurst machine · *Harvey & Peak · 1883–1900 · Metal, glass · 61 x 48.3 x 26.7cm · NT 1231069 · ‡ 1977*

Above · Sir William George Armstrong, 1st Baron Armstrong of Cragside (1810–1900) with his Wimshurst machine in a print (NT 1230793).

Going the extra mile

In the digital age, the technology in our pockets can give us directions or tell us how far we have travelled. This is possible thanks to generations of scientists and inventors who developed more accurate ways to measure things such as changes in weather, time and distance. By the 18th century Britain was undergoing a road-building boom and accurate measurements were needed for mapping routes, planning military defence, and determining land-ownership and estate boundaries. Surveyors drew on an ancient invention known as a waywiser, which translated the length travelled by a wheel into a distance.

This wooden waywiser at Kedleston Hall was made by Richard Glynne (1681–1755), a mathematical instrument maker. It measured the distance travelled by a moving coach wheel in miles and furlongs, showing the results on a brass dial. The Georgian gadget could have been useful to the Curzon family, who obtained an Act of Parliament to divert the public road around their estate when they rebuilt Kedleston in 1769. KK

Kedleston Hall, Derbyshire · Waywiser · *Richard Glynne · 18th century · Wood, paint and brass · 11 x 35 x 20.5cm · NT 108615 · Purchased with the aid of a grant from the National Heritage Memorial Fund · ‡ 1986*

Which ball?

It looks a little like a disco ball, but was this large, glass globe once used to protect its owner's home? It was purchased by keen collector Frank Green (1861–1954), the owner of Treasurer's House, who believed it was a witch ball. Witch balls were hung in cottage windows as protective charms, and the shiny glass surface was meant to reflect and neutralise the 'evil eye' of passing witches. The belief that a witch could inflict death or illness simply by looking at a person or animal was widespread. Glass witch balls were produced in various sizes and were still popular in the 19th century.

Frank Green is thought to have purchased at least three witch balls. He gave two to the Victoria and Albert Museum in London, which experts now think are actually late 19th-century Christmas baubles. This large glass ball still hangs at Treasurer's House, which was given to the National Trust in 1930. Green meticulously arranged the property's contents and allegedly warned that, if changes were made to the room layouts, he would return to haunt the building. KK

Treasurer's House, York · Witch ball · *Probably 19th century · Glass · 33cm (diameter) · NT 592934*

Gazetteer of National Trust Places

For full details of every National Trust property, including further information about collections, opening times, events and facilities, please visit the National Trust website (www.nationaltrust.org.uk) and the National Trust Collections website (www.nationaltrustcollections.org.uk).

A la Ronde, Devon · Unusual 16-sided cottage built, decorated and furnished by the Parminter cousins. The collections, which reflect their extraordinary craft skills and their European travels, include seaweed pictures, inlaid furniture, a 'cabinet of curiosities', a miniature library, a feather frieze and a magnificent shell-encrusted gallery and staircase.

Anglesey Abbey, Cambridgeshire · Comfortable Jacobean-style home containing rich collections assembled by Huttleston Broughton, 1st Lord Fairhaven. These include statues, jewellery and an interesting clock collection, as well as Lord Fairhaven's suits, shoes and books.

Arlington Court and the National Trust Carriage Museum, Devon · An eclectic collection reflecting the history of the Chichester family, who lived on the estate for over 500 years. It includes over 3,000 shells, pewterware and model ships. Arlington is also home to the National Trust Carriage Museum, which cares for the most representative collection of British carriages in the country.

Bateman's, East Sussex · The former home of British author Rudyard Kipling, with a comprehensive collection of his family's books, personal belongings and souvenirs, including his Nobel Prize for literature, paintings from *The Jungle Book* and his Rolls-Royce motor car. In 1903 Kipling installed a turbine in the nearby watermill to generate electricity for his new home.

Beningbrough Hall, North Yorkshire · Italian Baroque mansion on an estate owned by the Bourchier family since Tudor times. Few of the original contents remain but art exhibitions are displayed in the gallery space. Original architectural features include outstanding wood carvings, while graffiti carved above a fireplace reveals a wartime love story.

Biddulph Grange Garden, Staffordshire · Garden created by Victorian plantsman James Bateman to house his collection of plants from around the world. Globally inspired architectural features include a stone sphinx, gilded dragons and seahorses. Bateman's Geological Gallery is a Victorian curiosity combining science and religion, using fossils to tell a story of creation.

The Bowder Stone, Borrowdale, Cumbria ·
Huge, house-sized boulder balanced improbably
on one edge. A ladder allows visitors to climb
the stone and admire the view, as people have
done since it was established as a tourist
attraction in 1798.

Buckland Abbey, Devon · Once owned by
Francis Drake, this remodelled Cistercian abbey
includes spectacular Elizabethan plasterwork in
the hall and staircase. It has a wide range of
objects associated with global travel, including
sea chests, model ships and a pocket globe.

Calke Abbey, Derbyshire · Baroque mansion
that reflects an era of the country house in
decline. It is home to extensive natural history
and taxidermy collections (including a crocodile
skull and albino blackbird), a beautifully embroidered state bed, fossils, ceramic pigs, toys, wax
seals and many other personal treasures.

Castle Drogo, Devon · A 20th-century castle
designed by architect Edwin Lutyens. The
collection reflects the taste of the Drewe family
and includes bespoke furniture in the custom-
built kitchen, fishing equipment, magnificent
tapestries, a 1906 dolls' house and a plethora
of electrical and household gadgets.

Castle Ward, County Down · An 18th-century
house of contrasts, featuring both Palladian and
Gothic Revival architecture. The published works
and famous microscope of scientist and writer
Mary Ward are on regular display. The property
is also home to a striking sequence of taxidermy
displays depicting boxing squirrels.

Chartwell, Kent · The principal residence
of Winston Churchill from 1924 to 1965. The
collection contains Churchillian memorabilia,
including paintings, family photographs, books,
maps, cigar boxes and velvet 'siren suits'.

Chastleton House, Oxfordshire · Jacobean
home with impressive Long Gallery and Great
Chamber. The collection includes a wonderful
range of objects, from copper carriage warmers
and Jacobean drinking glasses to a huge 72-rung
ladder, a slipper bath and a Bible reputedly read
by Charles I before his execution.

Chedworth Roman Villa, Gloucestershire ·
One of the grandest Roman villas in Britain,
Chedworth was rediscovered in 1863 and is
still home to the Roman snail, now a protected
species. As well as extensive mosaic floors, a
flushing toilet and bathhouses, there is a small
museum displaying a range of finds, including
hairpins, pottery, coins, tools and carved stone.

**The Children's Country House at Sudbury,
Derbyshire** · A collection of objects reflecting
the experience of childhood through the
centuries. As well as toys, games and dolls,
there are items relating to childcare, costume,
education, hobbies and popular pastimes.

Chirk Castle, Wrexham · Medieval castle that
was home to the Myddelton family for 400
years. The interiors were remodelled between

the 17th and 20th centuries and the collection contains items as diverse as a Japanese domed lacquer chest, Neo-classical furniture and significant English Civil War firearms.

Clevedon Court, North Somerset · A medieval manor house and ancestral home of the Elton family. The collections include local Eltonware pottery, images of the Industrial Revolution and ornate objects made from Nailsea glass, including rolling pins, pipes and walking sticks.

Corfe Castle and Estate, Dorset · A 1,000-year-old castle partially demolished in 1646 by the Parliamentarians during the English Civil War. A series of excavations since the 1980s has uncovered finds relating to life in the village and castle, including musket balls, coins and medieval pottery.

Cotehele, Cornwall · A Tudor house owned by the Edgcumbe family from 1353 until 1947. The collection includes arms and armour, tapestries, cushions commemorating a royal visit, a whale's jawbones and an ancient faceless clock.

Coughton Court, Warwickshire · Tudor house and home of the Throckmorton family since 1409. It holds a collection of Catholic treasures, including a protest painting (*Tabula Eliensis*, 1596), a cope reputedly worked by Tudor queen Katherine of Aragon, lace-making equipment and a tailored coat made in a single day.

Cragside, Northumberland · The first house in the world to be lit by hydroelectricity, built for inventor, engineer and manufacturer William Armstrong. The collection includes objects reflecting his scientific curiosity and experimentation, as well as electrical household gadgets, British art and natural history.

Dudmaston, Shropshire · A modest house built *c.*1695 and altered in the 1800s. It provides a classical setting for a collection of modern and contemporary art, including works by Ben Nicholson, Henry Moore and Barbara Hepworth. The collection also encompasses household and estate items, including Jacobean oak furniture, handmade wooden coracles and an enormous goblet known as the Fool's Glass.

Dunham Massey, Cheshire · Georgian house built in 1720–38 for the 2nd Earl of Warrington. It contains one of the largest collections in the Trust, featuring everything from pet portraits and an early silver egg-cup holder to toys and fancy-dress costumes, hair art and a large orrery (a model of the solar system).

Erddig, Wrexham · Country house with Neo-classical interiors and fine examples of 18th-century Chinese wallpaper. The collection contains paintings and photographs of former staff, an early car, ceramic fish-shaped tureens and a Victorian shower. There is also a historical 'Failures Gallery' of gifts and objects not considered worthy of display elsewhere.

Felbrigg Hall, Norfolk · A fine 17th-century house given with its contents to the National

Trust in 1969. Paintings and grand-tour souvenirs are presented alongside family treasures, including magic lantern slides, toys, books and an antique fire engine.

Gray's Printing Press, County Tyrone · A treasure trove of ink, wooden and metal type and printing machinery hidden behind an 18th-century shopfront in the heart of Strabane, once the famous printing town of Ulster and birthplace of the man who printed the American Declaration of Independence.

Greenway, Devon · Georgian house that was the holiday home of Agatha Christie, her children and grandchildren. It contains a variety of objects owned by the family, including books, watches, straw-work boxes, archaeological material, souvenirs of travel and Christie's collection of homeopathic medicines.

Greys Court, Oxfordshire · A 16th-century mansion and family home full of household items, furniture and Swiss stained glass. The grounds include the 14th-century Great Tower and a rare Tudor donkey wheel.

Ham House, Surrey · A grand Stuart house with original interiors and collections, including a rare Chinese teapot, 'sleeping chairs', lacquer furniture and a group of miniatures still displayed in their original closet.

The Hardmans' House, Liverpool · A Georgian terraced house, the former home and photography studio of Edward and Margaret Chambré Hardman. It preserves the contents of a working studio and the family's furniture and personal effects, as well as the photographic collection.

Hill Top and Beatrix Potter Gallery, Cumbria · Hill Top is a small 17th-century farmhouse, bought in 1905 by Beatrix Potter and featured in several of her illustrations. The Gallery, formerly the office of her husband William Heelis, currently displays the National Trust's collection of Beatrix Potter's artwork.

Hughenden, Buckinghamshire · Country home of Victorian prime minister Benjamin Disraeli, containing collections of personal memorabilia, royal and diplomatic gifts and political mementos. Hughenden was used by RAF map-makers during the Second World War and interactive displays reveal this hidden history.

Ickworth, Suffolk · Neo-classical house designed to house a remarkable art collection. It contains an outstanding collection of silver, fans, significant paintings, a hall table supported by snow leopards from the Hervey coat of arms, and two Georgian Privy Purses embroidered in gold and silver. The house has seen many technological improvements, including the installation of communication tubes and a rainwater-harvesting system.

Kedleston Hall, Derbyshire · An 18th-century house designed by architect Robert Adam. Highlights in the collection include furniture by John Linnell and Robert Adam adorned with sea-nymphs and dolphins, a portrait of housekeeper Mrs Garnett and a copy of her original guidebook. There are also objects collected by Lord Curzon during his travels in South Asia and the Middle East, arranged and displayed by him in his 'Eastern Museum'.

Killerton, Devon · Georgian house set in 6,400 acres of parkland, which also contains the Bear's Hut or 'Ladycott' and an ice house. It is home to a large and varied collection of dress and accessories from the 18th to the 20th century.

Kingston Lacy, Dorset · Grand Venetian palace in the Dorset countryside, home to the Bankes family for more than 300 years. The spectacular interiors include fine paintings, hangings of gilded leather, bronze sculptures of family figures, ornamental tortoises and the largest private collection of Egyptian artefacts in the United Kingdom.

Knightshayes, Devon · Victorian Gothic Revival house designed by William Burges. His imaginative design includes sculpture and gilded ceilings. It is home to furniture by Burges and the Heathcoat Amorys' Old Master paintings and Italian maiolica.

Knole, Kent · Tudor archbishop's palace and home of the Sackville family for 400 years. It has an internationally important collection, including paintings by Thomas Gainsborough and Peter Lely, rare royal furniture, a life-sized plaster statue of an owner's former mistress and the original manuscript of Virginia Woolf's *Orlando*.

Lacock Abbey and Fox Talbot Museum, Wiltshire · Exceptionally complete medieval nunnery converted to a house in the 1540s, with 1750s Gothick additions. The collections include work by photography pioneer William Fox Talbot, a book from the nun's library, 16th-century stone tables, and extraordinary terracotta statues made at Lacock.

Little Moreton Hall, Cheshire · Impressive timber-framed Tudor home. A small surviving collection includes heraldic glass, pewter and a large oak spice chest, as well as discoveries made during conservation and restoration works, from hundreds of protective burn marks (thought to be linked to folk superstition) to marbles and early tennis balls.

Llanerchaeron, Ceredigion · An 18th-century Welsh estate and collection, also home to the Geler Jones Collection of agricultural tools and machinery, horse-drawn vehicles and domestic objects amassed by a local saddler; and a collection of some 5,000 objects amassed by antiques dealer Pamela Ward.

Lytes Cary Manor, Somerset · Small medieval manor house lovingly restored by Walter Jenner in a 17th-century style. The collection contains unusual leather figures, a raised-work embroidered mirror frame and a quirky cabbage-leaf teapot.

Montacute House, Somerset · Elizabethan house built of honey-coloured stone. Features include plasterwork friezes, a wind porch and collections of samplers and tapestries, as well as an impressive collection of Tudor and early Stuart paintings on loan from the National Portrait Gallery.

Mottistone Estate, Isle of Wight · Elizabethan manor house set in Mediterranean-style gardens, former home of General Jack Seely, 1st Baron Mottistone, and his war-horse 'Warrior'.

Mount Stewart, County Down · Early 19th-century house with a fine collection of equestrian paintings and mementos of family and political life, from embroidered chairs to a gold Cartier cigarette case. It is set in a largely 20th-century garden created by Edith, Lady Londonderry. The Dodo Terrace is populated with creatures inspired by The Ark, a war-time social group hosted by Edith and her husband in London.

Nostell, West Yorkshire · A Palladian house built on the site of a medieval monastery. Contents include a beautifully furnished 18th-century dolls' house, one of the first longcase clocks made by John Harrison and striking Chinese wallpaper. It is also home to one of the best surviving collections of Thomas Chippendale's furniture, including an enormous apothecary table and a dressing table complete with original contents.

Nuffield Place, Oxfordshire · Comfortable home of William Morris, Lord Nuffield, founder of the Morris Motor Car Company. A modest and personal collection includes everything from the contents of Lord Nuffield's bedroom tool cupboard and a specially designed electric exercise horse to a policeman's truncheon, as well as an array of memorabilia and gifts.

Osterley House, Middlesex · Tudor home of Sir Thomas Gresham, re-modelled by Robert Adam in 1763–80 for the Child family. Its Adam interiors contain collections of furniture, paintings, tapestries and coins.

Petworth, West Sussex · Set within a significant 'Capability' Brown landscape, the house has one of the greatest picture collections in the National Trust (including works by Anthony van Dyck, William Blake and Titian). The lifelike wood carvings by Grinling Gibbons in the Carved Room feature everything from wooden sheet music and instruments to a playful cat chasing a bird.

Powis Castle and Garden, Powys · Medieval castle remodelled by generations of the Herbert family with magnificent paintings and furniture, a rare Roman marble cat and a collection of objects brought from South and East Asia to Powis Castle by the Clive family.

Quarry Bank, Cheshire · One of Britain's greatest industrial heritage sites, showing how a complete working community lived. The diverse collection contains the business archive of the Greg family, who ran the mill, their possessions, and machines and other items relating to the cotton industry, many in working order.

Rufford Old Hall, Lancashire · A Tudor building complete with furniture, armour and a rare carved oak screen. Rufford is also home to the Philip Ashcroft Collection, preserving objects that reflect south-west Lancashire folk life, including tools, toys and household gadgets.

Shaw's Corner, Hertfordshire · Edwardian rectory that was the home of George Bernard Shaw from 1906 to 1950. Shaw's life as an author, critic, wit and political activist is reflected in the diverse collection, which includes representations of him on everything from bookends to puppets and a doorknocker.

Sissinghurst Castle Garden, Kent · Historic site purchased and restored by writers Vita Sackville-West and Harold Nicolson. Before it became a writer's residence, it had been used for a wide variety of purposes, from detaining French prisoners-of-war in the 18th century to serving as a base for the Women's Land Army during the Second World War.

Smallhythe Place, Kent · A 16th-century timber-framed farmhouse that was home to Shakespearean actress Ellen Terry until her death in 1928. It contains an important collection of theatrical costumes, memorabilia, a collection of friendship beads, and the death masks of Terry and her fellow actor Henry Irving.

Snowshill Manor, Gloucestershire · Cotswold manor restored by the architect, artist, collector and craftsman Charles Paget Wade. It contains an enormous and varied collection, including model ships, musical instruments, toys, bicycles and Samurai armour, as well as objects crafted by Wade.

Souter Lighthouse and The Leas, Tyne and Wear · The first lighthouse in the world designed to be powered by electricity, built in 1871 and decommissioned in 1988. The working machinery and collection give an insight into the life of lighthouse keepers and over a century of evolving technology.

Springhill, County Londonderry · Late 17th-century country house. The collection includes 18th- and 19th-century family portraits, a significant historic library and over 3,500 items of historic dress and textiles.

Sunnycroft, Shropshire · Late Victorian villa with a collection of objects from the Lander family, who lived here until 1997. It includes embroideries, the family medicine cabinet complete with contents, a Daimler car and objects from 20th-century domestic life.

Tatton Park, Cheshire · Neo-classical mansion that was home to generations of the Egerton family. The Egerton collections include books, paintings, natural history material, global collections and early cars. Tatton is managed by Cheshire East Council on behalf of the National Trust.

Townend, Cumbria · Yeoman farmhouse belonging to the sheep-farming Browne family for 400 years. This well-preserved home includes a 19th-century 'fitted' kitchen, household and farming items, bullet moulds, handcuffs, sheep plaques and a remarkable book collection, including chapbooks and unique or locally printed works.

Treasurer's House, York · Impressive townhouse restored and re-presented by wealthy industrialist Frank Green. His diverse collection of objects, furniture and antiques includes a Boulle writing table, wax portraits, a witch ball and a model ship with 132 miniature cannons.

Tyntesfield, North Somerset · Victorian Gothic Revival house with furnishings including a bronze 'throne', paintings, 19th-century books and thousands of domestic objects, from kitchen gadgets to ice skates and picnic sets. Throughout the house are carved motifs inspired by local wildlife and the surrounding countryside.

Waddesdon Manor, Buckinghamshire · Built for Baron Ferdinand de Rothschild in the 1870s to display his collections and to entertain. It is home to one of the world's finest collections of French art, including Sèvres porcelain, 18th-century furniture, and 17th- and 18th-century paintings and tapestries. Waddesdon is managed by the Rothschild Foundation (a charitable trust) on behalf of the National Trust.

Wallington, Northumberland · House remodelled in the 18th century. The collection includes family portraits, dolls' houses, needlework panels, a fantastical sleigh and a cabinet of curiosities with fossils, stuffed birds and a porcupinefish.

Wightwick Manor, Wolverhampton · Late Victorian Old English house with Aesthetic Movement-influenced interiors. Features Pre-Raphaelite pictures, including works by Rossetti, Millais, Elizabeth Siddal and Burne-Jones, as well as William De Morgan tiles and Morris & Co. stained glass, wallpapers, textiles and furniture.

Woolsthorpe Manor, Lincolnshire · A 17th-century farmhouse that was the childhood home of Isaac Newton. The collection includes a reconstruction of his reflecting telescope, a snuffbox made from the tree that allegedly inspired the theory of gravity, and sketches on the walls believed to be by Newton. Visitors can explore Newton's discoveries further in the hands-on Science Centre.

Compiled by Katie Knowles

Index

Acknowledgements

The author is immensely grateful to those who contributed entries to this book: Helen Antrobus (Assistant National Curator), Emma Campagnaro (Property Curator, Dunham Massey), Katherine Carter (Property Curator, Chartwell), Hannah Mawdsley (Property Curator, Ham House), Stephen Ponder (Cultural Heritage Curator), Alice Rylance-Watson (Assistant National Curator) and Harvey Wilkinson (Cultural Heritage Curator).

We would also like to acknowledge the many other members of National Trust staff who have made this book possible. Thank you to all the curators, Collections & House teams, property staff and volunteers who suggested objects for inclusion, assisted with research queries and shared their knowledge of and enthusiasm for these fascinating objects. Thanks to Emile de Bruijn, Nathalie Cohen, Nancy Grace, Sally-Anne Huxtable, Gabriella de la Rosa, Caroline Schofield, Heather Smith and Clara Woolford for advice on various entries.

Sincere thanks to Christopher Tinker, the National Trust's Publisher for Curatorial Content, for commissioning this book and overseeing the editing, design and production; and David Boulting, Editor

in the Cultural Heritage Publishing team, who copy-edited the texts with meticulous attention to detail, and undertook additional proofreading and picture research. We are grateful to Matthew Young for his wonderful cover design; Patricia Burgess for proofreading the book; Christopher Phipps for the index; and Richard Deal at Dexter Premedia for the origination. We would also like to thank photographers Leah Band, John Hammond and Dara McGrath, who travelled to properties across England, Northern Ireland and Wales, and to the property teams for supporting photography shoots.

Special thanks go to Tarnya Cooper, Rachel Conroy, Tate Greenhalgh, Christo Kefalas and James Rothwell for their advice, encouragement and support during the proofing stages; Alison Dalby for stimulating discussions about unexpected objects; and Laura Barker Wood and Heather Caven for support with collections information queries.

The National Trust gratefully acknowledges a generous bequest from the late Mr and Mrs Kenneth Levy that has supported the cost of preparing this book through the Trust's Cultural Heritage Publishing programme.

Picture credits

Pages 2, 12, 14, 33, 40–1, 47, 48, 49, 53 (and cover), 57 (bottom), 58–9, 60, 61, 68, 71 (and cover), 72, 78–9, 80, 86, 94–5, 98 (and cover), 100 (all), 101, 102, 103, 120, 122, 123, 126, 127, 130–1 (and cover), 132 (and cover), 133, 136 (and cover), 138, 140, 141, 142–3, 145 (and cover), 158–9, 160 (both), 162, 166–7, 170, 178, 178–9, 180, 181, 186, 193 (and cover), 196 © National Trust Images/Leah Band · 4–5, 112–13, 114 (all), 115 (all) © National Trust/Peter Muhly · 6, 13, 22, 25, 34, 54, 67, 175 © National Trust Images/Andreas von Einsiedel · 8–9, 44 (left) © National Trust Images/Paul Harris · 10, 64–5 (and cover), 174, 184–5 © National Trust Images/James Dobson · 16 ©National Trust Images/Geoffrey Frosh · 18, 26 © National Trust Images/Nadia Mackenzie · 21 © National Trust/Simon Harris · 23, 192 © National Trust Images/ Cristian Barnett · 27 (and cover) © National Trust/ Susanne Gronnow · 29 © National Trust/Sophia Farley · 30, 31 © National Trust Images/Mark Bolton · 36 © National Trust/Mike Howells and Roger Johnson · 37 (and cover) © National Trust/Claire Reeves · 38 (and cover) © National Trust/Andrew McGregor · 42, 44–5 (and cover), 46 (and cover), 55, 56 (and cover), 74, 75, 88, 91, 110, 116–17, 128, 129, 146, 147, 153, 172, 173, 194, 195, 197, 198, 202 (both) © National Trust Images/John Hammond · 50, 51 © National Trust Images/John Millar · 52, 87 (and cover), 144 © National Trust/Karen George · 57 (top) ©

National Portrait Gallery, London · 62, 85, 154–5, 190, 191 (all) © National Trust Images/Dara McGrath · 66 (and cover) © National Trust Images · 69 © National Trust · 70 © National Trust Images/Jon Bish · 73, 137, 149 © Alamy Stock Photo · 76, 106, 151, 168–9 (and cover), 183 (top), 207 © National Trust/Robert Thrift · 77 © National Trust Images/Robert Thrift · 81 © Chronicle/Alamy Stock Photo · 82, 83 © National Trust Images/David Brunetti · 90, 188 © National Trust Images/Chris Lacey · 92–3 © National Trust Images/David Garner · 96 © National Trust/Elizabeth Ogilvie · 97 (and cover) © National Trust Images/Matthew Antrobus · 104, 105 © National Trust Images/Rod Kirkpatrick/F Stop Press · 108 © National Trust/Rachel Nordstrom · 109 © National Trust Images/ Nick Carter · 111 (and cover) © Waddesdon Image Library, Mike Fear · 118 © National Trust Images/Ian Blantern · 119 © National Trust Images/Richard Pink · 125 © National Trust Images/Nick Guttridge · 134 © National Trust Images/Roger Coulam · 135 © KGPA Ltd/Alamy Stock Photo · 143 © National Trust/Anne Moore · 148 © National Trust/Clare Conybeare and Sarah Kay · 150 (and cover) © National Trust Images/Andrew Haslam · 157 © National Trust/Nick King · 161 © National Trust/Nathalie Cohen · 164, 165 Dalek image © BBC/Terry Nation 1963. Licensed by BBC Studios; Images: © National Trust Images/Leah Band · 167 © National Trust/David Presswell and Anne Chapman · 171 © National Trust/Maxine Scott · 177 © National Trust/Sue James · 182 © National Trust Images/Pete Tasker · 183 (bottom), 203 © National Trust/ Colin Liddie · 189 © National Trust/Stephen Shepherd · 200 © Tatton Park/Cheshire East Council · 201 © Tatton Park/Cheshire East Council/Peter Spooner · 204, 205 © National Trust/Andrew Patterson

Published in Great Britain by the National Trust, Heelis,
Kemble Drive, Swindon, Wiltshire SN2 2NA

National Trust Cultural Heritage Publishing

ISBN 978-0-70-780462-0

A CIP catalogue record for this book is available from the British Library.

10 9 8 7 6 5 4 3 2 1

Publisher: Christopher Tinker
Project editor: David Boulting · Proofreader: Patricia Burgess
Indexer: Christopher Phipps · Cover designer: Matthew Young
Page design concept: Peter Dawson, www.gradedesign.com

Colour origination by Dexter Premedia Ltd, London
Printed in Wales by Gomer Press Ltd on FSC-certified paper

MIX
Paper from
responsible sources
FSC® C114687
FSC
www.fsc.org

Unless otherwise indicated, dimensions are given
in centimetres, height x width x depth

‡ Indicates objects accepted in lieu of inheritance tax
by HM Government and allocated to the National Trust

Discover the wealth of our collections – great art and
treasures to see and enjoy throughout England, Wales
and Northern Ireland. Visit the National Trust website:
www.nationaltrust.org.uk/art-and-collections
and the National Trust Collections website:
www.nationaltrustcollections.org.uk

THE AUTHOR

Katie Knowles is Assistant National Curator for Engagement
at the National Trust. She specialises in interpretation and
has contributed to content and publications on the Trust's
rich and varied collections. She previously worked as the
National Trust's Research Manager and held various
communications roles before joining the Trust's Assistant
Curator training programme. (Information about the other
contributors can be found on page 222.)

ALSO AVAILABLE IN THIS SERIES

*125 Treasures from the Collections
of the National Trust*
ISBN 978-0-70-780453-8

*100 Paintings from the Collections
of the National Trust*
ISBN 978-0-70-780460-6

50 Great Trees of the National Trust
ISBN 978-0-70-780461-3